I Can't
Believe
They Said
That!

A book that furnishes no quotations is no book—it is a plaything.
— **THOMAS LOVE PEACOCK**

I like a book that leaves me smiling or shocked.
— **BEA ARTHUR**

A smart person knows what to say. A wise
person knows whether to say it or not.
— **THE DALAI LAMA**

*Guaranteed to shock! Offend! Titillate!
And . . . inform!*

I Can't Believe They Said That!

The Book of Outrageous Comments, Quips, and Zingers

BOZE HADLEIGH

LYONS
PRESS

Essex, Connecticut

An imprint of The Globe Pequot Publishing Group, Inc.
64 South Main Street
Essex, CT 06426
www.globepequot.com

Distributed by NATIONAL BOOK NETWORK

British Library Cataloguing-in-Publication Information Available

Library of Congress Cataloging-in-Publication Data Available

ISBN 9781493074594 (paperback) | ISBN 9781493074600 (epub)

™
∞ The paper used in this publication meets the minimum requirements of American National Standard
for Information Sciences—Permanence of Paper for Printed Library Materials, ANSI/NISO Z39.48-1992.

To Ronnie

and in memory of Jerry Kunz

CONTENTS

INTRODUCTION

Gentle reader, prepare to use your eyebrow muscles.

One sometimes wonders if most celebrities reach a point where self-censorship, not to mention good taste, simply disappears? So many have said something mind-bogglingly stupid or pernicious or both. Though dumb people don't always know they're dumb, surely any public figure is aware of the kind of statements apt to alienate millions of fans. Or does fame blind them to repercussions?

This collection is fun—partly because someone *else* said that—also funny, shocking or outrageous, often surprising or appalling, occasionally wise or useful, and informative. Everyone knows the Cuban missile crisis resulted in President Kennedy forcing the Russians to remove their missiles from the island nation so close to Florida, but less publicized (outside Russia), Premier Khruschev in return forced the United States to remove from Turkey its missiles that had been within striking distance of Moscow.

Included here are politicians as well as movie and TV stars, cultural icons, millionaires, inventors, criminals, authors, pundits, sex symbols, royals, athletes, professional critics, gossip columnists, historical (and hysterical) characters, habitual liars, bigots of all stripes, and those on a first-name basis with God.

Thirteen chapters:

One. "Say What?" abounds with "Did X really say *that?*" quotes. As in, how dumb or brazen can a celebrity get?

Two. "Sex." Need one say more? (The shortest after-dinner speech: "It gives me great pleasure." End of speech.)

Three. "Money and Technology" includes amazingly shortsighted predictions from giants of technology back in the day. Money encompasses Cary Grant charging 25 cents per autograph, taxes, alimony, Vegas and gambling, Elizabeth Taylor marketing perfume as "romance," and huge disparities in the *Gone with the Wind* leads' salaries.

Four. "Sports" features Kobe, Graziano, and Yogi Berra, plus Ivana Trump on skiing backward while blindfolded and President Johnson declaring President Ford "played too much football with his helmet off."

Five. "Enduring Marriage" (pun intended). Ronald Reagan on the Oscar (hers) that ended his first marriage. Prime Minister Margaret Thatcher's husband Denis wore the family pants—ever see her in a pantsuit?—but he also pressed them. And Ryan O'Neal, more realistic than in *Love Story*, said divorce "means never having to say you're sorry again."

Six. "Personal Life" explores things and people in the home, from microwave ovens that one GOP politician deemed more dangerous than guns to Miss Piggy's advice to never eat more than you can lift. Food, dieting, household possessions and habits, family relationships, health, clothes, grooming—the kitchen sink?

Seven. "Pretentious or Stupid?" Or both. Fame often initiates a lifelong affair with oneself. Michael Jackson on being "godlike," the "artist formerly known as" Prince, Jerry Lewis threatening Joan Rivers with violence, John Lennon on being a genius, opera diva Maria Callas on wanting never to have friends, and Marlon Brando on having the dignity to carry 300 pounds.

Eight. "Showbiz," not as happy as it's cracked up to be. Gossip and gloating, how stars live, love, and sometimes work. Cary Grant on LSD, literally. Rivals, rumors (mostly true), and how unhappiness starts with wanting to be *happier*.

Nine. "Politics." Big names, big promises, and bigger lies and egos, backstabbers, scandals, cover-ups, bigots, boobs (domestic and foreign), –isms, allies and enemies, and as Harry Truman said, if you want a friend in Washington, get a dog.

Ten. "Pants on Fire!" Tinseltown lies. Media lies. Political lies—of course. Tabloid lies—redundant. Even a UN agency describing coffee as "possibly carcinogenic" despite mounting evidence to the contrary. Historians wishing to whitewash (no pun) Thomas Jefferson, insisting he had no offspring by his slave Sally Hemings.

Eleven. "Costars and Peers." "Can we talk?" Celebrity diss-and-tell. Steve McQueen, glad about James Dean's death. "Control freak" Lucille Ball. Aunt Bee versus Andy Griffith. Sean Connery compared to an

Easter Island statue. Male and female celebs on and sometimes hitting on sex symbols Marilyn, Raquel, and Farrah. In ancient Greece the word for *actor* was the same as for *liar*.

Twelve. "Critic-sizing." Catty colleagues but also paid critics. An editor who thought *The Diary of Anne Frank* wouldn't sell copies, a reviewer who felt children wouldn't like *Alice in Wonderland*. Talent agents who told truck drivers Elvis and Rock Hudson to forget showbiz (keep your day job, boys). Actress/politician Glenda Jackson admitting most people have a book in them and that's where it usually should remain.

Thirteen. "Hyp, Hyp, Hypocrisy!" Where to begin? Washington? Hollywood? Televangelists? Image is one thing; the person behind the show of show business—spelled *bu$iness*—is often another. Said Abe Lincoln, "If I were two-faced, would I be wearing this one?" Publicity-seeking moralists who privately behave immorally. Secretly gay figures who publicly rant against gay people and equal rights (that's why outing was invented). Hypocritical leaders and actors—"Hypocrisy, thy name is Hollywood."

Happy reading!

1

Say What?

Honesty would be to Michael Jackson what daylight is to Dracula.
— playwright **ROBERT PATRICK**

✳

I ignore stupid jokes about cheapskate Scots. The worst is the Scottish pedophile who tells the kiddies to go easy on the candy.
— **SEAN CONNERY**, who donated over $1 million to the Scottish International Educational Trust, which he cofounded

✳

Medium well.
— comedian **W. C. FIELDS**, when asked by a female reporter how he liked children

✳

If men had to have babies, they would only ever have one each.
— **PRINCESS DIANA**

✳

Women are nothing but machines for producing children.
— **NAPOLEON BONAPARTE**

✳

After finding out what Robin Williams went through mentally and physically, I could mostly sympathize with his suicide. Except for the effects on his own children.
— **JANICE MCGOFF**, ABC-TV executive

Being a woman, I have long been for the right to choose. But definitely not China's example. Their one-family, one-child law [1980–2016] results in aborting countless future girl babies so that the parents can try again and perhaps get a boy.

— **ASTRID LINDGREN**, Swedish author
of the Pippi Longstocking books

✳

That reminds me, I need to pick up my laundry.

— movie mogul **JACK WARNER** to his assistant
on being introduced to Madame Chiang Kai-shek,
First Lady of Taiwan (the Republic of China)

✳

Peasant under glass.

— **PRINCE PHILIP**, husband of Queen Elizabeth II,
referring to the preserved remains of
Mao Zedong, a major Beijing tourist sight

✳

If you stay here much longer, you'll all be slitty-eyed.

— **PRINCE PHILIP** to a group of British
students during a royal visit to China

✳

That's one world-class bigot we're finally rid of.
. . . He was immune to criticism. It's not as if he
could have been sacked or impeached.

— antiroyalist writer **BEVERLEY SMITH** on
the 2021 death of Prince Philip, 99

For half a century, our gracious queen has retained
her dignity amidst family scandals, her sense of duty
during falling standards, and the same hairdo.
— **HONOR BLACKMAN** (*Goldfinger*)

✵

Anne Heche claimed she was straight till her first and only
lesbian relationship. Then straight again. Some people
actually believed that illogical statement. In truth, there are
women in this town who know that Anne went both ways.
— Hollywood publicist **RONNI CHASEN**

✵

Outside of the killings, we have one of the
lowest crime rates in the nation.
— **MARION BARRY**, mayor of Washington, DC

✵

She grew up in Graceland and moved to England, but Lisa Marie
Presley behaved in the manner of what Americans call white trash.
— UK journalist **DESMOND DAVIES**

✵

They're bringing out a Frank Sinatra doll—
$9.95, assault and battery not included.
— producer/writer **DOMINICK DUNNE**, who
contemplated suing Sinatra for A and B

Some people create happiness wherever they go. William
F. Buckley creates happiness whenever he goes.
— *Newsweek* editor **SARAH PETTIT**

[My] sworn enemy.
— **BOB BARKER** on fellow animal activist Betty White in
2009 after they differed on whether an elephant at the LA
zoo should be transferred. Barker threatened to boycott the
Game Show Network awards if White showed up; she taped
her appearance so that he could participate in person.

Playwright **CLARE BOOTHE LUCE**, stepping
aside in a doorway: Age before beauty.
Writer **DOROTHY PARKER**, walking
through: Pearls before swine.

On hearing that haughty Clare Boothe Luce was polite
to her inferiors: "Wherever does she find them?"
— **DOROTHY PARKER**

Ding, dong, the Holocaust denier is dead. Better late than never.
— actor and talk-show host **CHARLES GRODIN** on the
2020 death at age 101 of Hutton Gibson, Mel's father

Waiter goes up to a table of Jewish mothers
and asks, "Is anything all right here?"
— comedian **RODNEY DANGERFIELD** (born Jacob Cohen)

✴

I don't think anybody should write his
autobiography until after he's dead.
— producer **SAMUEL GOLDWYN** (earlier, Samuel Goldfish)

✴

To touch means instant death. Anyone caught will
be prosecuted to the full extent of the law.
— Indiana **POWER STATION SIGN**

✴

Baseball is 90 percent mental. The other half is physical.
— **YOGI BERRA**

✴

I'm glad we don't have to play in the shade!
— golfer **BOBBY JONES** on being told it was 105° in the shade

✴

He must have been a marvelous shot.
— **NOËL COWARD**, upon hearing that a not very
bright producer had shot himself in the brain

✴

That's a part of American greatness: discrimination. Yes, sir.
Inequality, I think, breeds freedom and gives a man opportunity.
— Georgia governor **LESTER MADDOX**

I don't like Mexican pictures. All the actors
in them look too goddamn Mexican.
— movie mogul **JACK WARNER**

I think the handsomest actor in pictures was Gilbert
Roland. If he hadn't been from Mexico, he could have been
up there with [Clark] Gable. He had the sexiest bedroom
eyes, a killer smile, and he was drenched in "it."
— **LUCILLE BALL**, who married Latino
Desi Arnaz. *It* was a euphemism for *sex appeal*,
back when the word sex wasn't freely used.

I remember when that book came out about lesbian
nuns. People were scandalized. I'd assumed most
nuns were lesbian, nonpracticing or otherwise.
— novelist **ANNE RICE**

Hollywood mythology always promoted heterosexual
love and romance. I very much like romance, but after
my one such sexual experience, I was disappointed.
. . . Also very sure and happy I was gay.
— **ANONYMOUS IRANIAN ACTRESS** living in France

All women love semi-rape. They love to be taken.
— James Bond creator **IAN FLEMING** in the
1962 novel *The Spy Who Loved Me*

No, no. What if they were not as good as me?
What would I do with those imbeciles?
— ballet star **RUDOLF NUREYEV** to *60 Minutes*
on why he didn't want to be a father

✳

Can I sue the pope?
— **ELIZABETH TAYLOR**, upon being condemned
in the Vatican newspaper for "erotic vagrancy" after
breaking up a second marriage in a row

✳

Apart from some of his twisted opinions, John Paul
II has the crooked posture of a jumbo shrimp.
— comedian **RICHARD BELZER**

✳

Joan Crawford had perfect posture, but it was rather
intimidating. She looked as if she'd swallowed a yardstick.
— **GLENN FORD**

✳

HOLLYWOOD PAPARAZZO: "If you retired
from acting, what would you do?"
RIVER PHOENIX, smiling: "I could lose all self-
respect and become a freelance photographer."

✳

I wish I could sue the *New York Post*, but it's
awfully hard to sue a garbage can.
— **PAUL NEWMAN**

Never trust a smiling reporter.
— New York mayor **ED KOCH**

✳

How can you support a closeted mayor who barely
acknowledges that AIDS exists? He's almost as bad
as Ronald Reagan, who at least isn't gay.
— AIDS activist **LARRY KRAMER** on Ed Koch

✳

I once heard a Canadian say that the Australians are a friendly
and virile group. He added, "And the men are nice, too."
— magazine editor **LEONARD KNIFFEL**

✳

I don't like country music, but I don't mean to
denigrate those who do. And for the people who
like country music, *denigrate* means *put down*.
— BOB NEWHART

✳

Me on Broadway? Seriously? . . . I don't know anything
about music. In my line, you don't have to.
— ELVIS PRESLEY

✳

If life was fair, Elvis would be alive, and all
the impersonators would be dead.
— JOHNNY CARSON

His kind of music is deplorable, a rancid-smelling aphrodisiac.
— **FRANK SINATRA** on Elvis Presley

✳

On a positive note, I'll say at least he did not molest little *girls*.
— African American singer **NANCY WILSON** on Michael Jackson

✳

I've known a lot of dumb actors. . . . But from my experience, singers are even dumber.
— ICM agent **ED LIMATO**

✳

I love you, Spain!
— **WHITNEY HOUSTON**, opening her concert in Lisbon, Portugal

✳

I figured a Caucasian was a gay Chinese.
— attributed to **ELVIS PRESLEY**

✳

I don't even know what street Canada is on.
— gangster **AL CAPONE**

✳

Generally, I think America is America.
— **IVANA TRUMP**

✳

I once spent a year in Philadelphia. I think it was on a Sunday.
— **W. C. FIELDS**

I know British actors who are openly gay in London
but in the closet in Los Angeles. This says worlds
about the difference between the two cultures.

— Australian **RICHARD WHERRETT**, founding
director of the Sydney Theatre Company

✳

Alfred Hitchcock was like a eunuch. For one thing, he was
a voyeur. Terrified of sex but dying to watch or peep. He was
fat and squishy and the most asexual man I've ever known.

— secretly bisexual UK actor **JAMES MASON**, who
costarred in Hitchcock's *North by Northwest*

✳

It's a scientific fact that if you stay in California,
you lose one point of your IQ every year.

— author **TRUMAN CAPOTE**

✳

Hedda Hopper was a mental defective. She wore corrective hats.

— actor **STEWART GRANGER** on the
Hollywood gossip columnist

✳

The only "genius" with an IQ of 60.

— **GORE VIDAL** on painter Andy Warhol

✳

In the next episode of Anna Nicole Smith's reality series, she
talks about the worst four years of her life. Third grade.

— **JOAN RIVERS**

School seldom teaches what you want to know. Two things
I had to learn as an adult: What did "Howdy doody" mean?
How-do-you-do. And why did Howdy Doody have 48 freckles
on his face? Because there were 48 states in the union then.
— **CONCHATA FERRELL** (*Two and a Half Men*)

✳

Paris ain't much of a town.
— baseball icon **BABE RUTH**

✳

I was asked to come to Chicago because
Chicago is one of our 52 states.
— **RAQUEL WELCH**

✳

I pity any actor who gets second billing to Raquel Welch.
He's really getting third billing to her breasts.
— costar **EDWARD G. ROBINSON**

✳

Marilyn was a likeable sex symbol. Raquel is not. Unlike
Monroe, Welch is like a high school girl who thinks her
looks entitle her to act superior and ignore your feelings.
— **DICK VAN PATTEN** (*Eight Is Enough*)

✳

Gary Cooper has the longest dick in town
but no ass to push it with.
— fellow movie star and ex-lover
LUPE VÉLEZ, a.k.a. the Mexican Spitfire

A testicle with legs.
— critic **PAULINE KAEL** on British actor Bob Hoskins

✳

Lucille Testicle.
— **JOHNNY CARSON** on Lucille Ball

✳

I hated working with that bitch. She was the biggest bitch in the
business. Thank God I'll never have to work with her again.
— **TOM BOSLEY** (*Happy Days*) on Lucille Ball

✳

Remember those "Ronald Reagan Is a Lesbian" buttons?
Like what was that all about? *He* wasn't. Maybe his, like,
first wife . . . Jane something-man or man-something.
Like a real butch movie star. *Her*, not him.
— shock comic **SAM KINISON** on Jane Wyman

✳

The more one says "like," the stupider one sounds.
It translates to "I'm not sure." As in "I can't, like,
stand radishes." Or "It costs, like, $4.50." How did so
many people become so linguistically insecure?
— English instructor **JENNIFER LANE**

✳

You'll enjoy a jock-full-of-nuts special at lunchtime.
— **MOREY AMSTERDAM**, mispronouncing
"Chock Full o' Nuts," his TV show's sponsor

The noblest of all animals is the dog, and the noblest of
all dogs is the hot dog. It feeds the hand that bites it.

— wiener king **OSCAR MAYER**

✳

Dahling, I adore your cocksucker suit!

— **EVA GABOR** backstage, complimenting a
talk show guest wearing a seersucker suit

✳

Did you hear the Statue of Liberty got AIDS?
She got it from the Long Island Ferry.

— **BOB HOPE**, who later apologized for the "joke"

✳

Most people do think of me as just another pinko faggot,
a bleeding heart, a do-gooder. But that's what I am.

— **LEONARD BERNSTEIN**

✳

Of course O. J. Simpson did it and got away with it because of a
racially biased jury. Racism can work both ways . . . this proves it.

— **PAUL SORVINO**

✳

Slavery built the South. I'm not saying we should
bring it back. I'm just saying it had its merits. For
one thing, the streets were safer after dark.

— **RUSH LIMBAUGH**

Did you know there's such a thing as a coffee
enema? Imagine having one part of your body
that's awake all night. Especially that one.
— comedian **MARTY INGELS**

✳

[I wish you could be here to] see all these beautiful white people.
— **NANCY REAGAN** to Ronald in 1980 during a Chicago
campaign fundraiser, via an amplified phone hookup

✳

Only in America can a poor black boy like Michael
Jackson grow up to be a rich white woman.
— actor **RED BUTTONS**

✳

She sure got the short end of the stick. Like mothers don't
count. . . . Racially, you only read the result of Obama's father.
— ABC-TV executive **JANICE MCGOFF**,
referencing the president's underpublicized white
mother Ann Dunham, an anthropologist

✳

Texas has some proud history. Its Anglos forced secession
from Mexico because Mexico had abolished slavery.
Texas got into the US with the help of slaveholding
states. . . . It took a civil war for the US to abolish
slavery, after several other countries had, minus war.
— Texan **LARRY HAGMAN** (*Dallas*) in a *Japan Times* interview

Americans enshrine the Protestant work ethic because it makes money. . . . Americans are notorious for their love of money—their foreign policies have more to do with free trade than supporting freedom.

— UK politician **SELWYN LLOYD**

In the United States no one dares print or even say that Martin Luther King [Jr.] habitually cheated on his wife . . . and there is evidence.

— actress **MARIE-FRANCE PISIER** on French TV

An asshole.

— author **BOB THOMAS** on "National Rifle Association mouthpiece" and actor Charlton Heston

Why can't I say "nigger" when I mean one particular black who misbehaves? Blacks say it to each other often. Isn't that a double standard?

— *Lifestyles of the Rich and Famous* host **ROBIN LEACH** to *Beverly Hills (213)* columnist Richard Gully

There's too many people alive today. In the old days, war kept the population down. Now we have to rely on epidemics and starvation. War was more efficient. . . . Like World War II got rid of about 40 million people, and lots of them were Russian.

— shock comedian **SAM KINISON**

Death has a tendency to encourage a depressing view of war.
— US Secretary of Defense **DONALD RUMSFELD**

✳

A single death is a tragedy; a million deaths is a statistic.
— Soviet dictator **JOSEPH STALIN**

✳

He no play-a the game; he no make-a the rules.
— US Secretary of Agriculture **EARL BUTZ** in 1974
at the World Food Conference in Rome, commenting
on Pope Paul VI opposing population control

✳

The most normal man I know.
— **ELIZABETH TAYLOR** on Michael Jackson

✳

After he was acquitted of child molestation charges,
Michael Jackson called me up and said, "I'm innocent,
I'm innocent! I'm so happy! I feel like a kid again."
— JOAN RIVERS

✳

When I've felt unloved or been lonely, the fact that I'm well-
endowed has been a big comfort. Physically but also spiritually.
— DAVID CASSIDY

✳

To be loved is very demoralizing.
— KATHARINE HEPBURN

Girls have to learn that jealousy is not flattering.
It's the biggest motive for men killing their wives,
ex-wives, girlfriends, or ex-girlfriends.

— author and educator **EVE KOSOFSKY SEDGWICK**

✳

On the whole, women think of love and men of gold
braid or something of that nature. Beyond that, people
think only of happiness—which doesn't exist.

— French president **CHARLES DE GAULLE**

✳

Newcomer Marilyn Monroe will never make
moviegoers forget Rita Hayworth.

— 1948 **FANZINE PREDICTION**

✳

Marilyn Monroe was my dream lover . . .
and not only when I was alone.

— Russian ballet star **ALEXANDER GODUNOV**

✳

I was approached by more than one famous actress in
my heyday. . . . I wasn't lesbian, but I did have a crush
on Marilyn Monroe. I would never have said no to her,
and any reasonable husband would understand that!

— **GLORIA STUART** (*Titanic*)

✳

Education teaches us that a mind is a terrible thing to waste.
Showbiz teaches us that a waist is a terrible thing to mind.

— **BEA ARTHUR**

We can always call them Bulgarians.

— movie producer **SAMUEL GOLDWYN** when informed by a shocked employee that a play he'd just acquired, *The Children's Hour*, was about lesbians

✳

He was middle-aged and homely but a sex symbol. What I didn't realize was how good an actor Jonathan Frid was. On *Dark Shadows*, a convincing heterosexual vampire. But once our interview started, I knew he was gay. Frid didn't speak or move like Barnabas.

— gay interviewer/publisher **RICHARD VALLEY**

✳

Some people already dislike me. Why give them more ammunition?

— English actor **DENHOLM ELLIOTT**, gay and HIV-positive, whose widow outed him in a book

✳

After I at last did come out, I could walk around in public breathing freely and not having to look to my right, to my left, and behind me. How do you spell relief? O-U-T!

— actor **DICK SARGENT** (*Bewitched*)

✳

The press can be vicious when they smell a juicy headline. . . . You'd think I'd committed murder or some big sin! . . . I fell in love with a young man whose father was my ex-husband. That's all. In no way was it what they called it: *incest*.

— actress **GLORIA GRAHAME**, who married director Nicholas Ray and later his son Tony

It's sinful for a woman to be in broadcasting or in some business.
God made her to be a great cook, a great washer of things.
— falsetto singer **TINY TIM**

✳

At 14 I went to work at the Dairy Queen, wore a little Dacron
uniform. So the old guy in charge asks me to accompany
him to the back room, to show me something. . . . Well, he
was all over me, grabbed every body part he could! Till he
had to stop and wheeze. The guy had a heart condition.
I escaped the back room . . . and when I told my mother about it,
she said, "You know, I know his wife. So let's just not mention it."
— actress **MARCIA WALLACE** (*The Bob Newhart Show*)

✳

If you can't keep quiet, shut up!
— director **GREGORY RATOFF** to his crew

✳

Please take lost children to the Lion House.
— **SIGN** at the National Zoo, Washington, DC

✳

My biggest regret in life is saving David Frost from drowning.
— UK comedian **PETER COOK** on the UK TV interviewer

✳

Television has raised writing to a new low.
— film producer **SAMUEL GOLDWYN**

Technology . . . it rhymes with *proctology*. I stopped going to the movies when the movies started coming in to me. Half the fun was going *out* to the movies. If you want to stay indoors, settle for TV.
— **SYLVIA MILES** *(Midnight Cowboy)*

✳

If I wanted comic strips, I looked in the Sunday paper or a comic book. Now half of Hollywood's product is comic strips . . . cardboard heroes, boring villains. Superficial plots and suspense. Every bad guy wants to conquer the universe. Try conquering disbelief. . . . It was better on the page than it is on the screen, and it let you use your imagination.
— **KIRK DOUGLAS**

✳

So Michael Jackson turned himself part white. But now we're told he fathers all-white children?
— UK actor **JOHN RICHARDSON**

✳

[Michael Jackson] cut off his nose to spite his race.
— singer **MARVIN GAYE**

✳

Marvin's last name was really Gay. He added an *e* 'cause he didn't want folks thinking he was gay. . . . Poor Marvin, his father shot him dead . . . father was a minister, got himself acquitted.
— actor **PAUL WINFIELD**

Racist this and racist that. So many allegations and complaints.
. . . You know what? Nature is racist. Figure it out.
— **JOHN MAHONEY** (*Frasier*) in 2017
to ex-agent Johnnie Planco

✳

You'd think by now they'd have invented mouse-flavored cat food.
— comedian **GEORGE CARLIN**

✳

Blondi is a good dog, a model dog.
— **ADOLF HITLER**, who hated cats and
eventually poisoned Blondi

✳

Heterosexual men who hate cats tend to be
bullies and contemptuous of women.
— psychotherapist Dr. **BETTY BERZON**

✳

[I know] why dogs are so wonderful—they
love women without their makeup.
— **CINDY WILLIAMS** (*Laverne and Shirley*)

✳

Tweety was a baby bird without feathers until censors made
him have feathers because he "looked naked." . . . Donald Duck
comics were banned from Finland because he doesn't wear pants.
— **CARTOON FACTOIDS** from the
Humane Society of the United States

Silly people are scared by the word *homo*. Dumb or smart, we're all *homo sapiens*, and most males are heterosexual but homosocial.

— bisexual poet **ROD MCKUEN**

Dating's not fun. Fun's what you might get at the end of it. Men don't date women for fun . . . or for conversation. For companionship and talking we got guys.

— **WAYNE ROGERS** (*M*A*S*H*)

My mother made me a homosexual.

— **UCLA GRAFFITO**. Another bathroom visitor added, "If I give her enough yarn can she make me one, too?"

Stick to driving trucks, kid.

— **ROCK HUDSON**, quoting one of several agents who felt he had no movie-star potential

You ain't goin' nowhere, son. You ought to go back to drivin' a truck.

— **JIM DENNY**, Grand Ole Opry manager who in 1954 fired Elvis Presley after a single performance

More than a few ignorant people have said Rita Hayworth was passing for white. In fact she was white, via a Spanish father and Irish mother. . . . Like some actresses, she exchanged her father's surname for her mother's.

— film historian **CARLOS CLARENS**

Maybe they don't look at us with their eyes. . . . Even Tom
Snyder, one of the smarter talk show hosts, calls us "nonwhite."
— *Skip E. Lowe Looks at Hollywood* guest **CESAR ROMERO**
on white Cubans, including Desi Arnaz and Andy Garcia

✳

If something is repeated often enough, it takes on
familiarity and then even a persuasive ring of truth.
— screenwriter **GARSON KANIN**

✳

The Gospels are believed not because they are
rational but because they are repeated.
— **OSCAR WILDE**

✳

My daughter said to me, "The most unfair thing about being
a girl is that God is a man—if She really is a man."
— singer **HELEN REDDY** ("I Am Woman")

✳

I believe in God; only I spell it "Nature."
— architect **FRANK LLOYD WRIGHT**

✳

When I lectured in Northern Ireland, I informed the audience,
so as to offend neither Catholics nor Protestants, that I was
an atheist. A woman raised her hand. "But would it be the
Protestants' or the Catholics' God you're not believin' in?"
— **QUENTIN CRISP**, British author

Regarding censors, prudes, and religious nuts, why
don't the 95 percent of us who aren't offended by
everything stop catering to the 5 percent who are?
— **GEORGE CARLIN**

✳

Religion is what keeps the poor from murdering the rich.
— **NAPOLEON BONAPARTE**

✳

Going to war over religion is basically killing each
other to see who's got the better imaginary friend.
— comedian **RICHARD JENI**

✳

A short summary of every Jewish holiday: They
tried to kill us. We won. Let's eat.
— Jewish comedian **ALAN KING**

✳

All creatures must learn to coexist. That's why the brown bear
and the field mouse can share their lives and live in harmony.
Of course they can't mate, or the mice would explode.
— **BETTY WHITE**

✳

Seagulls pluck food from air, water, and land. They follow boats,
dolphins, and plows in fields. They take fish from nets, sit on
pelicans, and feed under lights at night. They thrust their heads
inside seal vaginas to gobble umbilical cords after birth.
— Australian biologist and author **TIM LOW** (*The New Nature*)

Americans ask me why the Chinese zodiac has a Year of the Dog but no Year of the Cat? The cat was shamed at the Buddha's funeral, when all beings were supposed to be in harmony, after it sneaked away and killed a mouse.
— Cambodian Oscar-winning actor Dr. **HAING S. NGOR**

✳

The US is a violent place, perhaps more so for celebrities. John Lennon was the one Beatle to move there . . . killed in New York. . . . Haing Ngor survived the killing fields of Cambodia . . . killed in Los Angeles. And so on.
— UK actress **TANIA MALLET** (*Goldfinger*)

✳

My doctor warned me, "Bette, do you know that for every cigarette you smoke, you lose one minute of your life?" I said, "Doctor! What do I do now?" He said, "Never mind. You died eight years ago."
— impressionist **CHARLES PEARCE** as Bette Davis

✳

Smoking is one of the leading causes of statistics.
— **FLETCHER KNEBEL**, coauthor of the novel *Seven Days in May*

✳

A friend who meant well, which they always do, informed me, "Smoking will eventually kill you, you know." I replied, "I'm counting on it."
— TV host **GARRY MOORE**. It did.

I'm tall, I have a deep voice, sometimes I'm loud
and argumentative. If that makes me a man, fine. I
don't know that it makes me anything else.

— **BEA ARTHUR**, alluding to her perceived sexual identity

✳

It's the most ridiculous thing I've ever known. Whenever I hear
anything about that wedding, I shut my ears because it upsets
me so much. My boy would turn in his grave at the very thought
of what Lisa Marie has gone and done. He'd be hurting bad.

— manager Colonel **TOM PARKER** on the marriage
of Elvis Presley's daughter to Michael Jackson

✳

Please! Just too many so-called celebrities now. Very few
stars and few real celebrities . . . so little visual or vocal
difference between most under-forties. Send in the clones.

— **LEONARD NIMOY** ("Mr. Spock")

✳

Overpopulation, crowding, traffic. Problems big and small, so
many. Always something. But that's life, isn't it? Afterward . . .
no problems, I guess. Of course some aren't really *bad* problems.

— columnist **MOLLY IVINS**

✳

No problem is too big to run away from.

— **CHARLES M. SCHULZ**, creator of *Peanuts*

✳

Drive Carefully—We'll Wait

— New Mexico **MORTUARY SIGN**

2

Sex

Murder is a crime. Describing murder is not.
Sex is not a crime. Describing sex is.
— author **GERSHON LEGMAN**

✳

Indecent? If it's long enough, hard enough,
and in far enough, it's in decent.
— entertainer **BELLE BARTH**'s definition
of a censor's favorite word

✳

The first thrill of adultery is entering the house.
Everything has been paid for by the other man.
— writer **JOHN UPDIKE**

✳

It's awful, but cheating on your girlfriend isn't
as stimulating as cheating on your wife.
— actor **TROY DONAHUE**

✳

If I ever cheat on my wife, it'll be just oral sex. That
way, no possible pregnancy and my conscience can say it
wasn't really sex. Isn't that what one president said?
— actor **CHRISTOPHER PENNOCK**

✳

My definition of trust: two cannibals giving each other a blow job.
— comedian **RODNEY DANGERFIELD**

Linda Lovelace's grandmother died after
she went down on the *Titanic*.
— comedian **ALAN KING**, referencing the star of *Deep Throat*

✳

Women fake orgasms because men fake foreplay.
— talk-show host **VIRGINIA GRAHAM**

✳

I have faked an orgasm or two. Big deal. Men
can fake an entire relationship.
— novelist **JACKIE COLLINS**

✳

How can a real man tell when his girlfriend's
having an orgasm? Real men don't care.
— **NORM MACDONALD** (*Saturday Night Live*)

✳

Most men still don't know that *harass* isn't two words.
— actress **SUSAN STRASBERG**

✳

Three's company if you and your wife agree and you can afford it.
— comedian **DAVID BRENNER**

✳

When I got my first TV set, I stopped caring so
much about having a close relationship.
— **ANDY WARHOL**

Q: What's LXIX?

A: Sixty-nine, the hard way.

— TRIVIAL PURSUIT

✳

The idea of female erections . . . sounds made up.

— political journalist **DAVID HALBERSTAM**. MRI
studies of women watching pornographic videos
showed an increase in clitoral volume of 90 percent.

✳

How can you say no to a lady with 16 breasts?

— actor **CHARLES DURNING** on Muppet costar Miss Piggy

✳

With men, it's like I'm trying every color in the
jellybean jar to see what's going to taste good.

— RAQUEL WELCH

✳

I don't have fun times with married men. . . .
I mean to say, not *happily* married men.

— Swedish sex symbol **ANITA EKBERG**

✳

The main problem in marriage is that for a man,
sex is a hunger, like eating. If he can't get to a fancy
restaurant, he'll make for the hot dog stand.

— JOAN FONTAINE

Now at least I know where he is.

— **QUEEN ALEXANDRA**, after the burial of her womanizing husband, Edward VII, who in late middle age succeeded his mother, Victoria

✴

When women go wrong, men go right after them.

— **MAE WEST**

✴

Musical!

— **WINSTON CHURCHILL**, when asked by author W. Somerset Maugham what his sole gay experience was like, with handsome UK actor/composer Ivor Novello

✴

I lost my virginity to an older woman named Miss Bea Haven.

— secretly gay pianist **LIBERACE**. Insiders said it was probably a football player.

✴

There's a certain athlete who's become a woman. If he's still attracted to women, is he now a lesbian? Or if he's attracted to men now, was he gay or bi but untruthful then? Explain, please.

— **LOUIE ANDERSON** to Nikki Finke, *Deadline* blog founder and columnist

✴

The majority of male-to-female transsexuals have not had "The Operation." They've taken hormones, they've gotten breasts, but they haven't gotten rid of it. So, obviously they're not women. . . . It's closer to being a drag queen. Sorry, but that's the truth.

— photographer **HERB RITTS** to TV interviewer Carol Vitale

When I was up for the draft, the man interviewing me asked, "Do you like girls?" Had he been less, shall we say, Neanderthal, I would have replied, "Yes. I also like apple pie, but I don't want to sleep with it either."

— American transgender woman **CHRISTINE JORGENSEN** (born George)

✳

Did you hear about the three nuns who got expelled from the nunnery? They were caught doing pushups in the cucumber patch.

— comedian **TOM POSTON**

✳

The Pee-Wee Herman guy got arrested in Sarasota [in 1991] but was damn lucky. His sexual preference didn't come out then. Everyone assumed he was there for the straight porn, not the guys in the audience.

— publicist **JOE HYAMS**. Paul Reubens was also arrested in 1971 for the same "offense" in Sarasota, where his parents lived.

✳

Daddy warned me about men and alcohol, but he never said a *thing* about women and cocaine!

— bisexual stage star **TALLULAH BANKHEAD**

✳

I'm not addicted to cocaine. I just like the way it smells.

— **RICHARD PRYOR**

✳

No, dahling. I've no hard feelings about my ex-husband. . . . Truth to tell, that was the problem—precious few hard feelings.

— **TALLULAH BANKHEAD**

I went to Oxford on an organ scholarship. I enjoyed it so much, I applied for and got an extended organ scholarship.
— DUDLEY MOORE

✳

Jack [Benny] was at times naive. . . . I once asked him what he thought about oral sex. He thought a while, then said, "I think talking about anything controversial is a good idea."
— friend **GEORGE BURNS**

✳

I regret to say that we of the FBI are powerless to act in cases of oral-genital intimacy unless it has in some way obstructed interstate commerce.
— FBI director **J. EDGAR HOOVER**, who was very secretive about being gay

✳

Hell, it *is* part rattlesnake!
— President **LYNDON B. JOHNSON**, answering a CBS reporter who observed him urinating in dense undergrowth and asked, "Aren't you afraid a rattlesnake might bite it?"

✳

I never trust a man until I've got his pecker in my pocket.
— LYNDON B. JOHNSON

✳

More than one of [John] Kennedy's girlfriends has said her affair with the late president was a five- or seven-minute highlight of her life. . . . He disliked foreplay and bored easily.
— writer **KEN FERGUSON**

Dahling, any husband of yours is a husband of mine.
— **TALLULAH BANKHEAD** to Ginger
Rogers, who was not amused

✳

It's [factual] but virtually forbidden knowledge that for
the first six weeks or so, all humans in utero are female.
Thereafter, about half differentiate into males.
— Dr. **BETTY BERZON**

✳

Straight men are actually a minority. . . . Heterosexual
females and homosexual women and gay men added
together comprise 55 to 58 percent of the population.
— **J. D. SALVATORE**, female film producer

✳

I concentrated on my private parts, trying to *will* my
penis and testicles to grow. I even spoke to them.
But my mind failed me. I was humiliated.
— bisexual **MARLON BRANDO**

✳

A little Jewish guy is standing at a urinal in the men's
room when a big black guy runs in, whips it out, and starts
peeing next to him. The black guy says, "I just made it!"
The little guy says, "Can you make me one in white?"
— Jewish comedian **JAN MURRAY**

✳

Irony or tragedy? The only males who don't know what
smegma means are usually ones who have it.
— Jewish comedian **SHELLEY BERMAN**

It's peculiar, but in my semilimited experience, guys who are well-hung aren't that eager to disrobe, whereas at an orgy, one of the first guys to strip is usually, well, like a chipmunk, you know?

— actress **DEBRALEE SCOTT**

Well, it's no one I know.

— actress **CORAL BROWNE**, upon laying eyes on a 30-foot-tall golden phallus that dominated the stage set of the 1968 production of *Oedipus Rex* at London's National Theatre starring John Gielgud, who said, "I feel as if we should give the set designer a big hand."

What sex life? For me, an orgy is using more than one magazine.

— UK comedian **SPIKE MILLIGAN**

I heard the sweetest little story today. A man went to a dentist's office very late one night. The dentist let him in, popped him into the chair, and put a bib around his neck. "No," said the man, "it's my penis!"
The dentist said, "You've come to the wrong place, I'm a dentist."
"No, I haven't," said the man. "There's a tooth in it!"

— comic icon **BEATRICE LILLIE**, quoted in Bruce Laffey's biography *Beatrice Lillie*

Ladies, leave your clothes here and spend the afternoon having a good time.

— A **SIGN** in a laundry in Rome

Please leave your values at the front desk.

— A **SIGN** in a Paris hotel

✳

Ladies are requested not to have children in the bar.

— A **SIGN** in a Norwegian cocktail lounge

✳

I uphold traditional values.

— **RONALD REAGAN**. After wedding Nancy Davis in
1952, they had their first child seven months later.

✳

Nobody has any business being naked in bed
if they haven't decided to have sex.

— sex therapist Dr. **RUTH WESTHEIMER**. Though only
4′7″, she was a trained sniper during the 1948 Arab-
Israeli War. Her parents were killed by the Nazis.

✳

Mideastern men consider the West's obsession with breasts
infantile. The erogenous zone in the Middle East is a woman's hips.

— **OMAR SHARIF**

✳

In the male-designed Muslim paradise—apparently it says
this in the Koran—the men have sex with girls whose
virginity is constantly renewed. Can you believe it?

— political columnist **MOLLY IVINS**

Ninety-five percent of men's and women's bodies are the same. But as the French say, "*Vive la différence!*"

— Dr. **EMMETT STANTON**

You are a woman, aren't you?

— **PRINCE PHILIP** during a royal visit to Africa, upon receiving a gift from a female Kenyan

What the [UK] press doesn't reveal and almost never hints at is the prince's extramarital liaisons.

— writer **KEN FERGUSON** on Prince Philip's infidelities during his marriage to Queen Elizabeth

Marriage does tend to cure you of sexual longings—for each other.

— **SPENCER TRACY**, quoted by Jack Warner's assistant Richard Gully, who said the chronically alcoholic Tracy was all but impotent by the time he met "platonic girlfriend Katharine Hepburn," who became his nursemaid

I believe in romance. That's why I wrote it.

— **ROBERT JAMES WALLER**, author of *The Bridges of Madison County*. At 58 Waller left his wife, 56, for a woman 22 years younger.

They don't call me Tyrannosaurus sex for nothing.

— Senator **EDWARD M. KENNEDY**

He's been the only man in my life.
— **NANCY REAGAN**. Periodicals and publicity releases
on actress Nancy Davis said she dated many men.

By the time she was engaged, the studio had restored her
virginity. . . . Supposedly she'd been working so hard,
she had no time for men until Reagan came along.
— **PATRICIA LAWFORD STEWART**, widow of actor
Peter Lawford, on Nancy Davis, the future First Lady

The delight of a number of men and the regular lover of
alcoholic actor Robert Walker [of *Strangers on a Train*].
— **PATRICIA LAWFORD STEWART** on Nancy
Davis. She also claimed in print, during Nancy's
lifetime, that Davis was proficient at oral sex.

I have never come across anyone in whom the moral sense
was dominant who was not heartless, cruel, vindictive, log-
stupid, and entirely lacking in the smallest sense of humanity.
— **OSCAR WILDE**, who was gay, married, and a father

A very nervy Englishwoman once asked Kitty Carlisle
if she knew her husband Moss Hart was gay when she
married him? After a long, deadly silence Kitty said, "I was
aware he had the best taste of anyone I'd ever met."
— game-show host and panelist **GENE RAYBURN**

I am merely the canvas on which women paint their dreams.
— secretly gay or bisexual silent-movie star **RUDOLPH VALENTINO**, known as "the Great Lover." His two marriages were arranged by lesbian actress/producer Alla Nazimova, godmother to Nancy Davis (later Reagan).

✳

Marrying a bisexual has its challenges. There were times I didn't know which way to turn.
— torch singer **LIBBY HOLMAN** about actor Ralph Holmes, whom she wed in 1939. Holman was herself bisexual, in love with a DuPont heiress.

✳

I don't believe in bisexuals, Boze.
— **ROCK HUDSON** during a taped interview. My facetious reply: "You are not required to believe in them. They are not divine."

✳

Straights lump gays and bisexuals together, and yes, there is overlap. However, gays and straights are both prejudiced against bi's.
— bi UK actress **JUDY CARNE** (*Rowan & Martin's Laugh-In*)

✳

You know how a child who's punished for being left-handed sometimes learns to be ambidextrous to make life easier? I sometimes wonder if some young gays try and go bisexual to make life easier?
— actor **ROBERT GUILLAUME** (*Benson*), father of a gay son

It's insecurity . . . forever trying to make boys grow up to
be "straight," mostly through sports. . . . Hetero boys will
become heterosexual men regardless, and gay boys will become
homosexual men despite all the sports propaganda and shaming.
— gay actor **CHARLES NELSON REILLY**

✳

If I were slim, I'm sure I'd get asked about my sexual orientation.
But when you're heavy, they often assume you don't have one.
— actor **JAMES COCO**

✳

My puberty made me so uncomfortable I started eating. And
eating and eating. . . . Fat was like defensive armor. By the time I
was 10 or 11, I looked like a grown woman. Salesmen would come
to the door and ask if my husband was home. I said, "I'm nine!"
— comedic actress and game-show
panelist **MARCIA WALLACE**

✳

I had rather a bit of a crush on a boy when I was in
elementary school. It terrified me . . . until years later,
when I became convinced I really did like girls.
— James Bond **ROGER MOORE**

✳

A man who had kissed me once said it was very possible I was
a lesbian because I had no response to males, meaning him.
I didn't contradict him because I didn't know what I was.
— **MARILYN MONROE**

I discovered Dr. Anna Freud's [daughter of Sigmund] findings when she analyzed Marilyn during a week in London in 1956. According to Anna, Marilyn was bisexual.

— Dr. **LOIS BANNER**, Marilyn Monroe biographer

✷

I wouldn't mind being called a gay woman if it didn't sound like somebody tipsy. I'm a teetotaler. . . . I would not want to be called that other word [lesbian]. It sounds like someone from a communist country.

— **MARJORIE MAIN**, the movies' Ma Kettle, in the book *Hollywood Lesbians*

✷

Am I gay? Ha, ha, ha, aah . . . go ahead. Ask me anything you want. Clitoral or vaginal? Both, darling. I'll take anything I can get. Hah!

— **VALERIE HARPER**

✷

I'm not saying Walt Disney was a pederast. . . . His sex life, if any, beyond fathering two daughters was a secret. . . . I'm not the first to say he took a peculiarly strong interest in Annette Funicello, as a kid and then as a teen. If somebody really researched that, they might well discover something shocking. Or it may well have been just a huge, one-sided crush.

— actress **NOREEN CORCORAN**, sister of Disney child star Kevin Corcoran, to *Hollywood Reporter* columnist Robert Osborne

✷

Hey, it's one reason I always wear a little ribbon in my hair. I mean, just because I was on *The Dick Van Dyke Show*.

— actress **ROSE MARIE**

I think women are more sexually and mentally fluid . . .
and more accepting. Most women probably have a rather
surprising ability to be sexually pleasured by either gender.
— French actress **MICHELLE MORGAN**

✳

See, if your sex partner has a penis—and I don't judge, either
way—that is an impatient little critter . . . or not so little. Erect,
it wants satisfaction. After which it usually loses interest in you.
If your partner hasn't a penis, then said partner
can take more time to give you pleasure.
— sex therapist Dr. **SHIRLEY ZUSSMAN**

✳

You meet a guy you like, you have sex, he's terrific in
bed. You think maybe this one's a keeper. But if he
senses a whiff of love or your desire for commitment,
Mr. Average Likeable Guy is *outta* there.
— sometime-comedienne **FRANCESCA HILTON**,
daughter of Conrad and Zsa Zsa Gabor

✳

Men are like mascara. A little emotion, and they start running.
— screenwriter **HELEN DEUTSCH**

✳

When I was young, I used to think married couples had
more kids back then 'cause they loved each other more.
Nuh-unh. Some folks couldn't afford a condom supply
and hardly none could legally afford an abortion.
— comedienne **JACKIE "MOMS" MABLEY**

Father of 11 Fined for Not Stopping
— ***BOSTON HERALD* HEADLINE**
for a story about a car accident

The *real* solution for hunger and poverty is ignored. The poorest
people, inside and especially outside the USA, have the most
children. . . . It's *birth control!* Why is it so controversial?
— Hungarian playwright **GEORGE TABORI**

GROUCHO MARX (*You Bet Your Life* host):
Why do you have so many children?
MRS. STORY (contestant with 20 children):
Well, because I love children, and I think that's our
purpose here on Earth, and I love my husband.
GROUCHO: I love my cigar too, but I take
it out of my mouth once in a while.

Soon I'm going to meet somebody around my own
age, and she's going to be smart and beautiful,
and I'm going to date her daughter.
— BOB SAGET

Elvis likes them young. Very young. Underaged would do nicely.
— costar **GLENDA FARRELL**

All these . . . airhead young girl singers, mostly
blondes. . . . Do they *know* anything? They probably
think *Roe v. Wade* was a boxing match.

— PATTY DUKE

If men bore children, the right to abortion
would be enshrined in the Constitution.

— FAY KANIN, screenwriter and president of the
Academy of Motion Picture Arts and Sciences (AMPAS)

✳

For gay people in the 1950s, this was practically
a police state. You could be arrested in your own
home if you had an all-male pajama party.

— movie star **TAB HUNTER**, who was

✳

You blew it.

— secretly gay movie star **TYRONE POWER** in the
1950s to a UK talk-show host, whose lingering in the men's
room gave Power the wrong impression. Before exiting, the
hetero host replied, "That's exactly what I *didn't* do."

✳

Poor very rich George Michael, . . . looking for love in all
the wrong public places. Finally caught up with him.

— UK writer/archivist **GIL GIBSON**, referring to
Michael's arrest in a Beverly Hills men's room in 1998

I did *nothing* wrong!

— **ROBERT CLARY** (*Hogan's Heroes*), being interviewed by this writer for a cover story in *Not Born Yesterday*. Indeed. In 1994, in the same otherwise-empty Beverly Hills restroom as George Michael, Clary was entrapped by an attractive undercover cop.

Oh, Tallulah . . . the old days. Do you remember the minuet?

— actress **PATSY KELLY** to pal Tallulah Bankhead, who replied, "Dahling, I can't even remember the men I fucked!"

What's better than roses on your piano? Tulips on your organ.

— **LIBERACE**

She speaks French, too. Such a cunning little linguist.

— Dame **EDNA EVERAGE**, outing a Hollywood movie star years before she came out

Ronald Reagan's lesbian daughter-in-law is dead. Can I say that? Wasn't she?

— shock comic **GALLAGHER** on the 2014 death of Daria Palmieri, whose sexual orientation was not definitively established

Who was it said bisexuality doubles your chances for a date on Saturday night? Good to remember, in case you're desperate.

— **CARRIE FISHER**

Carrie and Penny [Marshall] are the best of friends,
very close. Closer than best friends. You could
guess from some of their photos together.
— journalist **LANCE LOUD**

✳

Marlon Brando was the first American star to come out
as bisexual. But don't expect him to confess that one of
his late son's male lovers was Marlon's lover first.
— talk-show host **SKIP E. LOWE**

✳

Straights think bisexuals are gay or "confused." . . . Gays
think we're sort of trying to pass. But some of us enjoy sex
so much, we don't limit ourselves to half the possibilities.
And if it's between consenting adults, so what?
— **DACK RAMBO** (*Dallas*)

✳

They're so handsome, I could be bisexual for them.
— **BURT REYNOLDS** to interviewer Barbara
Walters about Ryan O'Neal and other actors,
including the model for the Marlboro Man

I've always thought of David Cassidy as a latent heterosexual.
— **LIL SMITH**, *Teen Bag* magazine editor

Straight? I'm a vagitarian!
— **MIGUEL FERRER** (*NCIS: Los Angeles*)

"In spirit." and "Probably."

— **KURT COBAIN**'s answers to the questions "Are you gay?"
and "Are you bisexual?" In school his best friend was gay and
got gay-bashed, as did Cobain for having a gay friend.

✳

When a parent or teacher sends a teen to a psychiatrist because
the teen may be gay or lesbian, it inevitably backfires. . . . If we
lived in a heterophobic world and a teen was sent to a shrink
because of suspected heterosexuality, would that change anything?
All it could do is make the teen more secretive and paranoid.

— psychologist **CHARLES SILVERSTEIN**

✳

When I was in the military, they gave me a medal for
killing two men and a discharge for loving one.

— on the congressional cemetery tombstone of
Sergeant **LEONARD MATLOVICH**

✳

The most vocal homophobes are often closeted
homosexuals using bigotry as camouflage. . . . Tests prove
that homophobic men are more turned on to gay porn
than nonphobic straight men. . . . When a phobia becomes
an obsession, it reflects something deep inside.

— gay musical director **JOE LAYTON**

Sports figures often aren't the best fathers. . . . Dodgers manager Tommy Lasorda didn't acknowledge the AIDS death of Tommy Lasorda Jr., who officially died of "pneumonia volume depletion." Theatrical producer Joseph Papp acknowledged his son's death from AIDS and took part in AIDS fundraising activities, which Lasorda did not.
— **ANONYMOUS SPORTS BLOGGER**

✳

Died after a long illness.
— **VARIETY**, the "showbiz bible," not clarifying the AIDS death of singer Nat King Cole's son and Natalie Cole's brother Nat Kelly Cole, a writer, at 36 in 1995

✳

Family Heartbreak . . . After 8 Wives & 11 Children . . . Mickey Rooney's Agony: His Son Is Secret Gay!
— 1992 **GLOBE** tabloid headline. The son's mother, Rooney's fifth wife, was shot dead by her heterosexual male lover.

✳

I'll hit him when I see him. I'll punch him right in the nose, and I hope I have these rings on!
— **LUCILLE BALL** in the second issue of *People* magazine, furious at Marlon Brando for starring in the X-rated *Last Tango in Paris*

✳

Well, next time bring him along!
— an angry **ENGLISH HOSTESS** to Sir Noël Coward as he prematurely left a dinner party given in his honor with the excuse, "I must think of my youth, you know."

During a much-publicized fundraiser, . . . Richard Pryor publicly admitted he'd gone down on a guy. . . . I've read in a few places that he and Marlon Brando may have had a "thing." Could be.

— bisexual actor and father of five **ROBERT MORSE**

✳

Back when Tab [Hunter] and Tony [Perkins] were *real* close, the story was that Tab told Tony, "Someday you'll make a fine actor." And Tony said, "I already have. Several."

— actor **SAL MINEO**

✳

Folks who criticize others' sex lives are jealous or frustrated, . . . folks without a sex life or unhappy with the one they do have.

— **CHRIS FARLEY** (*Saturday Night Live*)

✳

There's a group of older people out there that will never accept [homosexuality], but there are a lot of empty cemeteries, and when they're filled, the world will be more tolerant.

— **A WRITER OF *ELLEN***, shortly after
the sitcom's cancellation in 2002

✳

Nearly two-thirds of American women can't say "vagina," sometimes using code words, as if it were shameful. . . . About half won't discuss their vagina, not even with a doctor. . . . Popular culture has made the penis acceptable and even humorous, but the vagina remains semi-taboo.

— sex therapist **SHIRLEY ZUSSMAN**

If a couple is mutually honest, they may ask each other postcoitus, "I'll tell you who I was thinking about if you'll tell me who you were thinking about?"

— author **GORE VIDAL**

✳

When turkeys mate, they think of swans.

— **JOHNNY CARSON**

✳

Flamingos and I have a great deal in common.

— *Jeopardy!* host **ALEX TREBEK** in 1987, ad-libbing to a factoid about flamingos only mating once a year

✳

Oh, well, buggers can't be choosers.

— **WINSTON CHURCHILL**, upon viewing a newspaper photo of the plain bride of a gay member of Parliament who unexpectedly wed in 1951

✳

Heredity.

— **PAUL LYNDE** on *The Hollywood Squares*, answering the question, "Nathan Hale, one of the heroes of the American Revolution, was hung—why?"

✳

In the ass.

— **A** *NEWLYWED GAME* **CONTESTANT**'s reply when asked, "Where is the strangest place you and your husband have ever gotten the urge to make whoopee?"

Sheba's like my wife, aren't you, sweetie?

— never-wed **JACK RUBY**, the secretly gay nightclub owner who in 1963 fatally shot Lee Harvey Oswald, the supposed lone killer of President Kennedy, to his pet dachshund Sheba

Cats can be stimulated to sexual activity by sounding the note *mi* of the fourth octave. By use of the same sound, kittens can be made to go to the bathroom. After puberty the sound becomes a powerful genital stimulant.

— **LEON F. WHITNEY** in Training You to Train Your Cat

If I was gay, would I have gained all this weight?

— UK actor **CLEMENT VON FRANCKENSTEIN**, who never married and whose "rock" was his cat Tallulah

I've been asked whether people who don't enjoy sex don't enjoy life? I'd say that to enjoy life, you must enjoy either food or sex or both. If you enjoy neither, then I don't know what's wrong with you.

— Dr. **PAUL MEEHL**, clinical psychologist

An amazing, and to some people hope-giving, statistic is that one of every six American adults agrees to have sex because they're too embarrassed to refuse!

— sexologist **JOHN TOWNSEND**

Freud was too hung up on sex. His shedding light on the subconscious was one thing, but he believed we come out of the womb sex-minded—supposedly subconsciously. No. Children are basically innocent, although not for as long as they used to be, thanks to the damned internet.

— NBC staff photographer **JOEY DEL VALLE**

When I got back, my mother asked me where I was. I told her I was playing with little Jimmy down the street.

"That's nice, Lucille. What did you play?"

I told her we played Milk the Cow.

"You played what?"

"We played Milk the Cow."

"Well," she said, putting her hands on her hips, "which one of you was the cow?"

"Jimmy was," I told her. "Besides, I couldn't be the cow. I don't have one of those things." That was the end of Milk the Cow.

— **LUCILLE BALL** on her early childhood in the book *Lucy in the Afternoon*

3

Money and Technology

Behind every great fortune there is a crime.
— **HONORÉ DE BALZAC**, 19th-century
French novelist and playwright

Remember when Ross Perot ran for president? As
if being super rich was reason and qualification
enough. At least *that* catastrophe was avoided.
— editor and author **MICHAEL DENNENY** in 2022

The richer they are, the richer they want to be.
Alternatively, they want power to equal their wealth.
— novelist **ANNE RICE**

✳

Huge wealth can erase murder. In 1966 Doris Duke, the world's
third-richest woman after the queens of England and Holland,
killed Eduardo Tirella, a talented gay man and war hero who
worked for her. . . . He was beginning a separate career as a
Hollywood set designer. But Duke felt she owned him. Shortly
after he informed her he was leaving her employ, she drove
a two-ton station wagon over him . . . and got away with it.
East Coast police labeled it an "unfortunate accident."
She bribed and paid her way out of it and gave millions to
local charity. . . . To her, millions were peanuts. She was
vicious, alcoholic, and desperately craved admiration.
— **RICHARD GULLY**, *Beverly Hills (213)* columnist
and aide to movie mogul Jack L. Warner

Whoever said money can't buy happiness
didn't know where to shop.
— writer and art collector **GERTRUDE STEIN**

✳

Nothing that costs only a dollar is worth having.
— cosmetics magnate **ELIZABETH ARDEN**

✳

What's the use of happiness? It can't buy you money.
— comedian **HENNY YOUNGMAN**

✳

A large income is the best recipe for happiness.
— JANE AUSTEN

✳

First, okay, a lot of the homeless want to be that way. . . .
Money would be wasted on them unless it's for food or booze
or drugs. . . . Second, they're not all really homeless. I see tents
all over the place. If you're homeless, your tent *is* your home.
— comedian **LOUIE ANDERSON**

✳

A bank is a place that will lend you money if
you can prove that you don't need it.
— BOB HOPE

✳

Gambling is a sure way of getting nothing for something.
— gambling guru **NICK DANDALOS** (Nick the Greek)

Practically guaranteed way to come home from Las Vegas
with a small fortune: Go to Vegas with a big fortune.
— Vegas comedian **SHECKY GREENE**

✳

The rich and famous should be judged differently. [Beverly
Hills] couldn't live vis the little people's tax money.
— cop-socker **ZSA ZSA GABOR** after her arrest

✳

Taxes are for the little people.
— hotelier **LEONA HELMSLEY** prior
to being jailed for tax evasion

✳

I of course admire the queen, . . . but why shouldn't she walk
about smiling? She's a multibillionaire and only recently began
paying income tax, in 1993, after public pressure had mounted.
— UK actor **ALAN BATES**

✳

My rackets are run strictly on American lines,
and they're going to stay that way!
— gangster **AL CAPONE**

✳

If you think nobody cares if you're alive, try
missing a couple of car payments.
— ANONYMOUS

Everyone is an estate sale waiting to happen.

— estate appraiser and "vintage" merchant **DUANE SCOTT CERNY**, author of *Selling Dead People's Things*

✳

I don't want it good. I want it Tuesday.

— studio chief **JACK WARNER**

✳

Money trumps romance, real or manufactured. This famous couple's publicity said they celebrated their 10th anniversary, when in truth he filed for divorce, with no explanation, a few days short of a decade. Why? In California the 10-year mark is crucial. . . . It affects "spousal support." A "long-term marriage" is 10 years. Romantic, huh?

— Hollywood columnist **JOE HYAMS**

✳

Perfume is the closest thing to marketing romance.

— **ELIZABETH TAYLOR**, whose White Diamonds was a best-seller

✳

What use could this company make of an electric toy?

— **WILLIAM ORTON**, Western Union president, declining in the 1870s the chance to buy the patent for the telephone

✳

Everything that can be invented has been invented.

— **CHARLES DUELL**, US Patent Office commissioner, in 1899

Man will not fly for 50 years.
— aviation pioneer **WILBUR WRIGHT** in 1901

✴

The cinema is a fad. It's canned drama. What audiences
really want to see is flesh and blood on the stage.
— **CHARLIE CHAPLIN**, ca. 1916,
before becoming a screen icon

✴

Air mail is an impractical sort of fad and has no place
in the serious job of postal transportation.
— **PAUL HENDERSON**, second assistant
US postmaster general, in 1922

✴

The most dangerous phrase in the language
is "We've always done it this way."
— Rear Admiral **GRACE HOPPER**

✴

Who the hell wants to hear actors talk?
— Warner Bros. cofounder **HARRY WARNER** in 1927.
Ironically, his studio introduced talking pictures.

✴

I have no fear that the screeching . . . sound film
will ever disturb our peaceful theaters.
— movie columnist **LOUELLA PARSONS**

✴

I think there is a world market for about five computers.
— **THOMAS WATSON**, IBM chairman, 1943

Computers in the future may weigh no more than 1.5 tons.
— *POPULAR MECHANICS*, 1949

✳

But what good is it for?
— **ANONYMOUS IBM ENGINEER** in 1968
on the recently invented microchip

✳

IBM stands for solving problems that can be overcome.
— **ANONYMOUS COMPUTER ANALYST** in the 1950s.
The 2001 book *IBM and the Holocaust* revealed how the
company helped provide the organizational machinery used
to transport millions of people to Polish Nazi death camps.

✳

There is no reason for any individual to
have a computer in their home.
— **KEN OLSEN**, president of Digital Equipment, in 1977

✳

Who in hell is going to look at those pygmy screens?
— MGM chief **LOUIS B. MAYER** on the future of television sets

✳

I fear the day that technology will surpass our human
interaction. The world will have a generation of idiots.
— **ALBERT EINSTEIN**

✳

My theory of relativity is don't hire 'em!
— movie mogul **HARRY COHN**

The biggest crooks are the oil company execs and their coconspirators, the dictators of oil-rich countries, unethically exploiting us because we overdepend on petroleum.

— actor **ORSON BEAN**

✳

I see my grandson infrequently and am not particularly close to him.

— oil billionaire **J. PAUL GETTY**, who initially refused the ransom for grandson J. Paul Getty III, whose ear kidnappers cut off. Not publicized at the time: Getty only agreed to pay the $1 million ransom as a loan to his son J. Paul Getty II, repayable at 4 percent interest.

✳

Clark Gable worked on *Gone with the Wind* for 71 days and received $120,000. Vivien Leigh as Scarlett O'Hara worked for 125 days and was paid $25,000.

— film historian **CARLOS CLARENS**

✳

SCTV's cast all helped write the show. Difference is, the actors got paid for their writing; the actresses didn't.

— entertainment writer **ANN STEVENS**

✳

I read where L. Ron Hubbard informed his friends, "I'm starting a new religion, 'cause it'll pay better than writing sci-fi." So he called it Scientology.

— actor **GEORGE NADER**, who published the gay sci-fi novel *Chrome*

Scientology isn't science or a real religion. . . .
Closeted homosexuals are among its biggest backers.
The "church" helps deeper-closet them, profitably
pairing them with female Scientologists.
— gay African American actor **PAUL WINFIELD**

✳

Back in the late '90s, the *New York Post* got hold of a confidential
agreement employees had to sign that worked for this movie-star
couple where the husband was the bigger star. . . . It specified
how much the employee would be fined if there was "disclosure"
to any one given individual, how much for each printed copy
of a periodical if the employee did an interview, and how much
if there was a US TV broadcast, also each rebroadcast. . . .
The fines were astronomical, clearly meant to intimidate.
The guy's a control freak, is obviously terrified of being
found out. Did I say *out*? Okay, sue me, dude.
— actor-turned-writer **JACK LARSON**
(Jimmy Olsen on TV's *Superman*)

✳

I would rather play "Chiquita Banana" and have my
swimming pool than play Bach and starve.
— orchestra leader **XAVIER CUGAT**

✳

The first million-dollar check to fight AIDS was given
by a Japanese philanthropist. The second by American
magazine publisher Malcolm Forbes, who recruited
Elizabeth Taylor to cloak his true sexuality.
— Australian theater director **RICHARD WHERRETT**

When a child quadruples her family's income,
some changes may be expected.
— former child superstar **SHIRLEY TEMPLE**, commenting
on occasionally bending her parents' will to hers

✳

Stella Stevens made a few movies for Fox before they
dropped her. A single mother, she posed nude for *Playboy* for
$5,000. Then Hugh Hefner decided to cut her pay in half
unless she worked as a "hostess" at the Playboy Mansion. . . .
Before the photos were published, Stella landed a contract
with Paramount. She begged Hef not to run the photos
and jeopardize her position at that studio. He refused.
Stella didn't set out to be a blonde sex symbol. Her aim was
directing, a notion which each and every studio head laughed at.
— publicist **ANDREW FREEDMAN**

✳

The Gabor sisters boil down to high-class whores. Twenty
or so husbands between the three, and just one child. They
were very careful. Beyond the 20 legal lovers, there were
dozens of others. Their mother sometimes pimped them.
— agent and writer **JIM PINKSTON**

✳

Living in the lap of luxury isn't bad, except you
never know when luxury is going to stand up.
— ORSON WELLES

Aristotle Onassis owned Monaco's casino. To drum up publicity and more business, he ordered Prince Rainier of Monaco to marry a Hollywood star . . . a blonde. Marilyn [Monroe] was considered but . . . way too sexy. Grace Kelly had a pristine image, though in reality she slept with her leading men. As Princess Grace, she missed acting but wasn't allowed to return to it. She found little love in Rainier, overweight and widely rumored to be bisexual. . . . She became an alcoholic and, like Princess Diana several years later, died in a car crash.

— biographer **C. DAVID HEYMANN**

✳

Thanks to marrying rich men they never had to call her the bouncing Czech.

— columnist **RICHARD GULLY** on Ivana Trump

✳

Yesterday my wife was at the beauty shop for two hours—and that was just for the estimate.

— HENNY YOUNGMAN

✳

Well, he was quite wealthy, and I've always liked to shop. . . . It's very expensive to be me.

— ANNA NICOLE SMITH, widow of an octogenarian, explaining how she spent $6.7 million on jewelry, clothes, and homes during their 14-month marriage

✳

Because Hollywood's real homophobic, and after we got married, we could get credit cards.

— eventually openly gay comedian **STEVE MOORE** on why he married a lesbian (for 15 years)

Next-best Bond to Sean Connery was the second one, the
Australian [George Lazenby] in *On Her Majesty's Secret
Service*. . . . Decades afterward, the role was almost offered
to another Aussie, but the producers worried he was too
close to his male "assistant," regardless of having a wife,
which all male movie stars do. . . . The money men didn't
want rumors coming out about a gay James Bond.

— columnist **LEE GRAHAM**

∗

Some of O. J. Simpson's employers, including that car-
rental company, knew about his wife-beating. It was
a well-known regular thing, like his jealous rages. . . .
As long as they could benefit, they didn't care. Money
is the great justifier, for employers and employee.

— *Newsweek* editor **SARAH PETTIT**

∗

Listen, to stop the alimony, I'd remarry the broad
myself—if I didn't have to live with her.

— **GEORGE C. SCOTT**

∗

Change is inevitable. Except from a vending
machine or in a stale marriage.

— **LARRY KING**

∗

It's the rooster that does all the crowing, but
it's the hen that delivers the goods.

— Texas governor **ANN RICHARDS**

Talk is cheap, . . . and in Hollywood it's always on sale.
— ROBERT MITCHUM

✳

One of the main reasons people talk is
to camouflage their thoughts.
— Olympic gold medalist and
plastic surgeon Dr. **JOHN EMERY**

✳

The Jews, as a class violating every regulation of
trade established by the Treasury Department and
also department orders, are hereby expelled from the
department within 24 hours from receipt of this order.
— Order 11, issued in 1862 by General (later president)
ULYSSES S. GRANT, who erroneously believed Jewish
cotton speculators were abetting the black market for cotton.
Grant's military district, or "department," comprised parts of
Tennessee, Mississippi, and Kentucky. The resulting protests moved
Abraham Lincoln to order Grant to rescind the order. Wife Julia
Grant stated Ulysses had "no right to make an order against
any special sect." Grant was the only POTUS ever arrested: In
1872, he was caught speeding—in a horse-drawn carriage.

✳

I bought stock in ITT . . . a go-ahead, progressive company.
— stockbroker **STEVE TURNER**. Among other
dealings, ITT lent support to Nazi Germany and helped
overthrow Chile's elected government in the 1970s.

New Zealand and Australia introduced the minimum
wage in the 1890s. Britain did in 1909. . . . The US
waited until 1938 to provide a minimum wage via the
Fair Labor Standards Act, . . . 25 cents an hour.

— economist **HOWARD BOARDMAN**. New Zealand and
Australia were also the first nations to give women the vote.

✳

Being an actor or actress does not pay enough to live on for
most. You only hear about the rich ones. . . . You don't hear that,
then and now, quite a few actors of both sexes have to support
themselves—they're typically good-looking—through prostitution.

— showbiz columnist **RADIE HARRIS**

✳

Cary Grant's reality was far from his eventual image. He
grew up in dire poverty. . . . When finally he became a
father, he would order baby food in bulk to save money,
. . . even then complaining that it was overpriced.

— *Bewitched* actor **DICK SARGENT**, who said he
declined Grant's advances when they worked together

✳

I saw Cary Grant charge fans 25 cents for each autograph. He said
the money went to charity. . . . I don't know if I believe that one.

— *North by Northwest* costar **EVA MARIE SAINT**

✳

My wife asked for plastic surgery. I cut up her credit card.

— **RODNEY DANGERFIELD**

Cheap? I have a friend who's cheap. He found out it takes 10 dollars a year to support a kid in India, so he sent his son there.
— **RED BUTTONS**, comedian and Oscar-winning actor

✳

Some film "superstars" are enduringly mean [cheap]. Our Hollywood correspondent has seen a lesbian movie star attempting a discount on her movie ticket, arguing about her VIP card. . . . An even higher-paid male star, not lesbian but neither heterosexual, tried to get into a summer movie free, by virtue of who he was.
— **ANONYMOUS BRITISH *PHOTOPLAY* EDITOR**

✳

Don't buy one more vote than necessary. I'll be damned if I'll pay for a landslide.
— millionaire **JOSEPH P. KENNEDY**, in a "humorous" telegram to his son, future president John F. Kennedy

✳

Vegas is all about money, man. Back in '52, it was prejudice and worrying what their white customers might think.
— **SAMMY DAVIS JR.**, who in 1952 swam in a whites-only pool at the New Frontier Hotel. After he emerged, the hotel drained the pool.

✳

People are too easily taken in by televangelists who are filthy rich and often hypocrites. . . . Someone once said if life was fair, the only way you could get AIDS would be by contributing money to two-faced televangelists.
— author **CONNIE CLAUSEN**

Pat Robertson is the kind of Christian that
makes me glad there are Muslims.
— author **CHRISTOPHER HITCHENS**

✳

Persistent rumors that Joan Crawford did a porn flick
as a struggling chorus girl. Nothing ever surfaced. So
either the rumors were untrue—from enemies—or
Metro [MGM] bought up all the existing prints.
— Hollywood columnist **LEE GRAHAM**

✳

Sometimes it's not about money; it's a kink or showing
off. I believe Chuck Connors [*The Rifleman*] was straight.
. . . I owned footage of him screwing another man. . . .
Somehow the LAPD found out, . . . raided my home,
confiscated the "evidence," and never returned it! I
wonder how many times they've watched that film.
— literary agent **JIM PINKSTON**

✳

If the average guy is horny enough, he'll screw anything. It's
just that he won't admit to anything too out of the ordinary.
— actor and male pin-up **TROY DONAHUE**

✳

I was in Bangkok one time, and the management sent up
some guy. To my room! Some gay guy who wanted to . . .
Anyway, in that part of the world if you're blond, male
or female, they think you're up for grabs, sexually.
— **DAVID SOUL** (*Starsky and Hutch*)

There are 1,049 federal statutes that provide benefits, rights, and privileges to individuals who have the legal right to marry. . . . Those 1,049 benefits, rights, and privileges amount to *respect*. . . . Demanding legalized gay marriage is . . . not about "copying them." It is about money and rights.
— screenwriter/activist **LARRY KRAMER**, before the 2015 legalization of gay marriage

✴

When I was growing up, two great things about being gay were not having to get married and not having to be drafted into the army. Now you have thousands of gays fighting for all that!
— actor **RON VAWTER** (*Philadelphia*)

✴

Marriage is the only contract between two people that can't be dissolved by mutual consent. It requires the state's permission. Sounds kind of dictatorial to me.
— never-wed **GEORGE TOBIAS** (Mr. Kravitz on *Bewitched*)

✴

I vant a man who's kind and understanding. Is that too much to ask of a millionaire?
— multimarried media fixture **ZSA ZSA GABOR**

✴

Mother alvays said never to take candy from a stranger. Get real estate instead.
— multimarried **EVA GABOR** (*Green Acres*)

✴

When a man gives you a gift, honey, you will pay for it.
— PEARL BAILEY

I'm a vunderful housekeeper. Every time I
get a divorce, I keep the house.
— **ZSA ZSA GABOR**

✳

Marriage contracts back then were about property,
. . . with the husband legally branding the woman and
their offspring *his*. . . . Women couldn't earn a living
outside of prostitution—*no* economic security. In
the modern world, husbands are a dying need.
— **RUE MCCLANAHAN** (*Golden Girls*)

✳

It took longer to make one of Mary Pickford's contracts
than it did to make one of Mary's pictures.
— producer **SAMUEL GOLDWYN**

✳

I had it in my contract that if [W. C.] Fields got drunk on
the set, I stopped everything and had the guy ejected from
the lot. It was a pleasure pouring him outta there.
— **MAE WEST** on her *My Little Chickadee* costar

✳

I don't cheat on my wife because I love my house.
— actor **DEAN STOCKWELL**

✳

I tried to remarry my ex-wife, but she
realized I was after my money.
— **DEAN MARTIN**

Cary Grant and Clark Gable often met on December 26 to exchange monogrammed gifts they didn't want. . . . The cheapest stars were usually Republicans like Gable and Grant, Liberace, Fred MacMurray.

— columnist **LEE GRAHAM**

✳

Retire? Why? Age 65 is the first day of the rest of your life savings.

— Los Angeles writer and archivist **JIM KEPNER**

✳

The networks, they're always nervous, . . . afraid to lose any viewers, a sponsor, any profits. . . . Now I'm "Mexican."

— Cuban **DESI ARNAZ** on the nationality CBS reassigned him as *I Love Lucy*'s Ricky Ricardo after Cuba went communist in the late 1950s

✳

It's a hell of a move. Makes the guy look pretty crass or desperate, whichever way you look at it.

— singer **JOHN DENVER** on David Bowie's issuing bonds supported by the anticipated worth of future royalties from his songs, in 1997

✳

I don't go with that. This director made a movie, it didn't get the big audience he wanted, so he kept yelling, "Racism." What kind of example is that?

— African American actor **HOWARD ROLLINS**

4

Sports

I can ski backwards on one ski. And blindfolded!
— IVANA TRUMP

✳

I wouldn't go racing down a snow-covered mountain in a car with good brakes, much less alone on skis. Are you nuts?
— photographer **KENN DUNCAN**,
when asked if he'd like to learn

✳

Skiing did kill off Sonny Bono. . . . Guess it can't be all bad.
— PHIL SPECTOR

✳

Americans call their baseball championships the *World* Series, yet no other country is involved. Delusional, eh?
— Hollywood-based UK actor **JOHN ABBOTT**

✳

Skateboarding idiots, . . . or is that redundant?
— CARRIE FISHER

✳

I quit school in the fifth grade because of pneumonia.
Not because I had it but because I couldn't spell it.
— boxer **ROCKY GRAZIANO**

✳

Bad Spellers of the World, Untie!
— GRAFFITO

Gerald Ford played too much football with his helmet off.
— President **LYNDON JOHNSON** on the
nonintellectual future president

✳

It seems almost too good to believe that a president of one
leading institution has common sense enough to do something
to help rid college life of heathen cruelty and terror.
— a 1905 letter by an **ALUMNUS OF COLUMBIA
UNIVERSITY** after his alma mater, among other
schools, temporarily banned football

✳

The Stronger Women Get, the More Men Love Football
— 1994 book title by **MARIA BURTON NELSON**. Its
subtitle: *Sexuality and the American Culture of Sports*.

✳

Soccer requires skill. . . . No, it requires skills, plural. Football
requires brute strength and some skill. Hmm. Leave it at that.
— sportswriter and soccer specialist **GRANT WAHL**

✳

The thing that most puzzles me about the States is why cricket and
rugby haven't caught on here. Cricket . . . absolutely delightful!
— Englishman **BORIS KARLOFF**

✳

I did not pay three pounds fifty just to see
half a dozen acorns and a chipolata.
— UK actor/playwright **NOËL COWARD** after viewing a male
nude scene in the rugby-themed play *The Changing Room*

If a man watches three football games in a row,
he should be declared legally dead.
— humorist **ERMA BOMBECK**

Our generation was sports, not drugs. So maybe we're a bit
naive. I heard tell Woody Hayes thought uppers are dentures.
— ex-football player and -coach **BO SCHEMBECHLER**
on his fellow ex-player and -coach

Death tends to sanctify, especially premature or violent
death. But back when Kobe Bryant was stuck in that sexual
harassment mire, his peers only extended so much sympathy.
He wasn't a joiner, had a snobbish attitude. . . . Several players
felt he should be brought down a few pegs. . . . Sports is about
teamwork. Even if another's a better player, no one wants to
feel lower than the next player. . . . Aloof doesn't pay off.
— sports journalist **YVON PEDNEAULT**

Nappy-headed ho's.
— shock-radio host **DON IMUS**'s description of
Rutgers University's female basketball team in 2007. He
had to apologize, and MSNBC dropped his show.

If a man cares about his daughter's health and well-
being, he encourages her to play a sport. . . . For boys it's
often overemphasized; for girls, underemphasized. Sports
contribute measurably to girls' confidence and self-esteem.
— actor **DAVID HEDISON** (*The Fly*)

If sports and exercise keep you young, how
come athletes have to retire by 35?
— **NELL CARTER**

✳

It can end up discouraging at a gym. I go to keep in
shape. When I'm done exercising, on my way out,
I'm faced with vending machines that the sadistic
gym owners have so prominently installed.
— actress **JANET MARGOLIN**

✳

The leading cause of injuries in older men is
them thinking they're still young.
— **BOB MACKENZIE**, music producer of the Oak Ridge Boys

✳

For his 106th birthday, his wife Joy had a new swimming pool
put in so he could do his laps every morning. On the first day,
Mr. Abbott, who'd been swimming for over a century but was
a little out of practice, climbed in and sank like a stone.
As he was fished out, he said, "Damn thing
doesn't work. Send it back."
— theater historian **MARK STEYN** on
producer/director George Abbott

✳

Think about it—some jugglers could simply
be schizophrenics playing catch.
— poet **ROD MCKUEN**

Now *there's* a Father's Day gift that'll go unused.
— columnist **RADIE HARRIS** on Tricia Nixon's 1968 gift
to President Nixon of a custom-made blue surfboard

Well, it's easier to steer.
— center square **PAUL LYNDE**'s reply on *Hollywood
Squares* when asked if multi-Olympic-gold-medalist
"Mark Spitz believes it's easier to swim nude."

Three kinds of people. Those who watch sports. Those who do
sports. Those not interested. . . . I think the best all-round sport is
swimming—the best exercise, and water in you and on you is vital.
— modeling agent **NINA BLANCHARD**

I fish, therefore I lie.
— **ANDY GRIFFITH**, taking off on
Descartes's "I think, therefore I am."

While playing golf today, I hit two good balls. I stepped on a rake.
— **HENNY YOUNGMAN**

White men play golf so they can dress up like pimps.
— **RICHARD PRYOR**

You ever watch golf on television? It's like watching flies fuck.
— comedian **GEORGE CARLIN**

When I want to play with a prick, I'll play with my own.
— **W. C. FIELDS**, after MGM chief Louis B.
Mayer suggested a round of golf

✳

Baseball's been called the national pastime. It's just
the kind of game someone deserves who has nothing
better to do than to try to pass his time.
— **ANDY ROONEY** (60 Minutes)

✳

I don't want to make the wrong mistake.
— baseballer **YOGI BERRA**

✳

The only thing dumber than a pitcher is two pitchers.
— baseball manager **TED WILLIAMS**

✳

I wonder if boxers harbor any unexpressed frustrations.
. . . For a living, they get to beat people up.
— press agent **BEEBE KLINE**

✳

He's so ugly, they ought to donate his face
to the World Wildlife Fund.
— **MUHAMMAD ALI** on boxer Joe Frazier

✳

He is phony, using his blackness to get his way.
— African American **JOE FRAZIER** on Muhammad Ali

Does anyone on this planet think sumo wrestlers are sexy? The, uh, costume sort of is . . . but not the guys bulging out of them. The hairdo's cute, though.

— **BONNIE TIEGEL**, TV producer

✳

In America, competitive sports are like war, minus the killing.

— **ANDY KAUFMAN** (*Taxi*)

✳

Howard Cosell got a tremendous amount of press and got to overshadow being a sports announcer. He courted controversy and created an arrogant personality cult. . . . In the long run, he wasn't good for sports, and when his excesses backfired on him, he began criticizing, even hating sports.

— sportswriter **HUGH MCILVANNEY**

✳

If Howard Cosell were a sport, he'd be roller derby.

— sportswriter **JIMMY CANNON**

✳

We invented tennis. . . . In the 1500s, we replaced using our palms with racquets. . . . Its name comes from *tenez*, meaning *take it*, and *love* or a *goose egg* is from *l'oeuf*, which means *the egg*.

— French actress **JEANNE MOREAU**

✳

Two cats at Wimbledon, watching a tennis match. The first one says, "The blond player has a strong backhand but a weak forehand and serves terribly." The second cat asks, "How come you know so much about tennis?" The first cat says, "My father's in the racket."

— comedienne **TOTIE FIELDS**

5

Enduring Marriage

A woman is the only thing I am afraid of
that I know will not hurt me.
— **ABRAHAM LINCOLN**

✳

Happiness is having your girlfriend's lipstick
the same color as your wife's.
— **PHIL HARTMAN**, whose wife fatally shot him

✳

The music at a wedding procession always reminds
me of the music which leads soldiers into battle.
— poet **HEINRICH HEINE**

✳

Most marriages don't add two people together.
They subtract one from the other.
— **IAN FLEMING**, creator of James Bond

✳

Unfortunately, most marriages can be
summed up as a hymn to him.
— UK actress **JUDY CARNE**, Burt Reynolds's first wife

✳

Skip it if you can. After you marry a woman, she'll make you
an expert on the kind of man she should have married.
— actor **RAY DANTON**

There are four major reasons marriages fail: money, sex, intellectual incompatibility, and only one bathroom.
— **BETTE DAVIS**, who had four husbands

✳

It does appear so.
— **LISA MARIE PRESLEY** in 2021, responding to the question "Did Michael Jackson [by marrying you] use you?"

✳

After you get married, you start wondering if everybody else has a better sex life.
— screenwriter **JEFFREY BOAM** (*Indiana Jones and the Last Crusade*)

✳

Some studies say married people live longer.
Not really. It only seems longer.
— **JERRY SEINFELD**

✳

The only really happy folk are married women and single men.
— writer **H. L. MENCKEN**

✳

One should always be in love. That is the reason one should never marry.
— **OSCAR WILDE**

Divorce? Never. But murder, often!
— Dame **SYBIL THORNDIKE**, when asked
if she'd ever considered divorce during her
lengthy marriage to Sir Lewis Casson

✳

Well, there were three of us in this
marriage, so it was a bit crowded.
— **PRINCESS DIANA** on television

✳

I married him for better or worse but not for lunch.
— the **DUCHESS OF WINDSOR** (wife of the ex-king
of England), whose busy social life was inviolable

✳

If you were my husband, I'd put poison in your coffee.
— Lady **NANCY ASTOR** to Winston Churchill, who
replied, "If I were your husband, I'd drink it!"

✳

My wife's an earth sign. I'm a water sign. Together we make mud.
— **RODNEY DANGERFIELD**

✳

We want playmates we can own.
— cartoonist **JULES FEIFFER** on why men marry

✳

Men marry so they can screw. For free. Women
screw so they can stay married.
— **CARRIE FISHER**

I married to have children, and I divorced
to not have a husband. *Comprende?*
— screen siren **VERONICA LAKE** to a Hispanic journalist

✳

HUSBAND: You don't have much up
there. Why do you wear a bra?
WIFE: Why do you wear briefs?

✳

Men are bigger but more insecure. What they fear from
women is being laughed at. What women fear from
men is being hit or killed. Basic stuff, people.
— poet **ROD MCKUEN**

✳

Years later, [producer] Robert Evans informed me he'd had a big
crush on me but hadn't done anything about it because he couldn't
get involved with a woman whose voice was lower than his!
— actress **SUZANNE PLESHETTE**

✳

It doesn't really matter who you marry. Next
morning she'll turn into someone else.
— **REDD FOXX** (*Sanford and Son*)

✳

I discovered that my first wife was a lesbian. That sort of
thing has a very discouraging effect on a young man.
— **ALAN NAPIER** (Alfred the butler on TV's *Batman*)

Homophobia has pushed thousands of ambitious or less brave men into acquiring wives as fronts. . . . If you don't marry someone you want and love, it's not a real marriage.

— writer and gay activist **LARRY KRAMER**

I had a lesbian friend whose wealthy father's will stipulated she must marry to inherit. So she did, and it worked out because *he* was gay, and they led their own separate lives.

— novelist **JACKIE COLLINS**

Bigots who say gay marriage threatens the institution of marriage ignore the fact that bad marriages are bad from the inside, not the outside.

— **DORIS ROBERTS** (*Everybody Loves Raymond*), pre-2015

During his publicity marriage to Elvis's daughter, she was spending more time with her ex-husband than Michael. And when they did that puff ABC interview together as marrieds, they arrived and departed in separate cars that night.

— publicist **HOWARD BRAGMAN**

One of my marriages was so short, I was afraid if we didn't wait, we'd have to give the wedding presents back.

— **TROY DONAHUE**. His ex was actress Suzanne Pleshette.

If the minister doesn't enunciate properly, it can sound like
"Do you take this woman for your awful wedded wife?"
— comedian **ALAN KING**

The only person who listens to both sides of a husband-
wife argument is the woman in the next apartment.
— **BROOKLYN PROVERB**

Cary Grant resented Paramount making him take a
wife and took it out on her. Several wives later, he was
still using his fists, . . . and one said if she'd stayed in
the marriage, she'd be dead, "in a grave dead."
— film historian **C. DAVID HEYMANN**

I left [Burt Reynolds] the day he threw me against
our fireplace and cracked my skull.
— **JUDY CARNE** (*Rowan & Martin's Laugh-In*)

I left Sean Connery after he bashed my face in with his fists.
— actress **DIANE CILENTO**

Sure, I've slapped Tina. . . . And there have been times when
I punched her without thinking. But I never beat her.
— **IKE TURNER** in his memoirs

I slapped my wife [Katherine DeMille, Cecil's adopted daughter] on our wedding night because she wasn't a virgin. I was so disappointed.
— ANTHONY QUINN

Men don't like criticism, even silent comparisons—a big reason they'd rather marry virgins.
— British actress **SUSANNAH YORK**

During Jim Brown's trial on domestic-abuse charges, his wife claimed she had given him permission to smash up her car with a shovel.
— *ESQUIRE* MAGAZINE

George C. Scott. Fine actor. Big drinker. Wife beater. What else do you want to know?
— actress **COLLEEN DEWHURST** on her ex in the book *Hollywood Babble On*

When a woman goes from married to divorced, she raises the intelligence quotient of both categories.
— LYNN REDGRAVE, whose then-husband impregnated their son's girlfriend

Is it female-chauvinistic to say all women marry beneath them? But so often, it's true!
— BETH HOWLAND (*Alice*)

I disliked married life, which gives the man more
status and power. It slots the wife—the former friend
and partner—into a restrictive role. I never legally
remarried so I could remain just Me, not Mrs. He.

— actress **STELLA STEVENS**

While dating, a cynical but important part of
your mind has to wonder how good of a weekend
father this potential ex-husband will make?

— marriage counselor **PAULINE BARHAM**

FIRST FEMALE: So what did you do on your date?
SECOND FEMALE: We went horseback riding.
FIRST FEMALE: Was it fun?
SECOND FEMALE: Well, yeah, until we ran out of quarters.

Marry an orphan—you'll never have to spend boring holidays
with the in-laws. . . . At most an occasional visit to the cemetery.

— comedian **GEORGE CARLIN**

The labor of women in the house certainly enables men to
produce more wealth than they otherwise could; and in this
way, women are economic factors in society. But so are horses.

— American writer/activist **CHARLOTTE
PERKINS GILMAN** in 1900

At every party there are two kinds of people: those who want to go home and those who don't. The trouble is, they're usually married to each other.

— advice columnist **ANN LANDERS**

✳

He and his third wife, [actress] Mayo Methot, were known as the Battling Bogarts. She was alcoholic and at times violent. . . . For some time after we met, Bogey feared for my safety. So did I! Later, I felt sorry for her.

— **LAUREN BACALL**, Humphrey Bogart's fourth and final wife

✳

The happiest marriage in Hollywood.

— **JOAN CRAWFORD** on friend and former star William Haines and Jimmy Shields, together 47 years

✳

Hollywood's Unhappiest Couple?

— **FAN MAGAZINE CAPTION** of a photo of William Holden and Brenda Marshall, who gave up her acting career to be (alcoholic) Holden's wife from 1941 to 1971

✳

"Till death do us part." And wouldn't you know, nowadays people are living a lot longer.

— TV star **MICHAEL LANDON**

✳

My ex-husband died last week. . . . You're only supposed to speak good of the dead. All right, then. My ex-husband died last week—*good!*

— comedienne **JACKIE "MOMS" MABLEY**

Never go to bed mad. Stay up and fight.
— PHYLLIS DILLER

✳

Desi [Arnaz] is a loser. A gambler, an alcoholic, a skirt-chaser . . .
a financially smart man but self-destructive. He's just a loser.
— ex-wife **LUCILLE BALL**

✳

I love Lucille, but when it came to choosing Desi, she might
have guessed. He was several years younger and a Latin Don
Juan who flirted with everyone. . . . They were on the brink
of divorce several times before and after their TV show.
— actress/dancer **ANN MILLER**

✳

Lucy told CBS she would only do *I Love Lucy*, not some
other show they wanted. . . . It was to keep her husband from
touring all over the country with his band. They'd be working
together full-time, and she could keep her eye on him.
— costar **MARY JANE CROFT**

✳

The reason our marriage works is we spend half the year together
and half apart. . . . A wife who tries to live through her husband
fails, or the marriage does, or it becomes a trial for both of them.
— ESTELLE GETTY (*Golden Girls*)

✳

Fonder. Wrong word. Absence makes the heart go yonder.
— AVA GARDNER

Happiness is having a large, loving, caring, close-knit family—in another city. . . . Contentment is knowing your wife's nearby, and so's the next meal.

— GEORGE BURNS

✳

When I first met George Burns, I could see he had what it took to become a star: Gracie Allen.

— fellow comedian **MILTON BERLE**

✳

My wife's over 60, and she still doesn't need glasses. She drinks right out of the bottle.

— HENNY "Take my wife, please" **YOUNGMAN**

✳

I'm an Irishman. I'd rather drink than fight.

— PAUL KELLY, who often played police officers, imprisoned in 1927 for manslaughter after fatally shooting his girlfriend's husband. In 1931 he married her; in 1940 she died in a car crash.

✳

My wife said when she was down in the dumps, she'd go shopping. I said, "Honey, I'm no tightwad. Try going to a dress shop."

— PETER FALK

✳

On our final anniversary, as a present, I cooked him a homemade meal. He said, as a present, he'd eat it.

— NELL CARTER (Gimme a Break)

Forget older men. Young guys are used to fast food and
eating out. . . . Old ones expect you to cook for them!
— comedienne **JUDY TENUTA**

✳

I begged Richard [Dawson] not to go to the States. You know
what happens to most British actors who go there? They finish
by playing butlers or opening fish-and-chip stands. With Dickie
it was worse: He became host of something called *Family Feud*.
— UK sex symbol **DIANA DORS** (born Diana Fluck)

✳

If it weren't for divorce, where would
coffee shops get their waitresses?
— writer **BUCK HENRY**

✳

I'm at this ritzy banquet . . . rich food. I belched,
couldn't help it. Guy to my right says about the broad
to my left, "How dare you belch before my wife?" I
apologized, said, "I didn't know it was her turn."
— comedian **RODNEY DANGERFIELD**

✳

I couldn't see tying myself down with a middle-aged
woman with four children, even though the woman
was my wife, and the children were my own.
— middle-aged writer **JOSEPH HELLER**

Have you ever seen a husband and wife dancing, where he's trim and well-groomed and she's got thinning hair and a belly? Aha!

— comedienne **JUDY TENUTA**

✴

This great man was married to a great many women. They're all flat now.

— **DON RICKLES** on the obese Orson Welles

✴

Why did Nixon see *Deep Throat* three times? He wanted to get it down Pat.

— **GRAFFITO** referencing the president and his wife

✴

If it comes to a divorce with Jane [Wyman], I think I'll name *Johnny Belinda* as corespondent.

— actor **RONALD REAGAN**, who disliked having a wife more successful than he. She won an Oscar for *Johnny Belinda*.

✴

I do, and I also press them.

— **DENIS THATCHER**, husband of UK prime minister Margaret Thatcher, when asked who wears the pants in the family. The antifeminist PM eschewed pants.

✴

If Clark had one inch less, he'd be the "queen of Hollywood" instead of the "king."

— **CAROLE LOMBARD**, Gable's third wife. A 1937 poll named Gable the king of Hollywood and Myrna Loy the queen of Hollywood. He remained the king for the rest of his career; Loy was only queen for a year.

Debbie Reynolds was indeed the girl next door.
But only if you lived next door to a self-centered,
totally driven, insecure, untruthful phony.
— ex-husband **EDDIE FISHER**, who claimed
she had no interest in sex with him

✳

Judy's first husband was older and boring. Her second was
older and gay, but he believed in her talent, helped beautify
her, and successfully directed her on-screen. . . . Vincente
Minnelli preferred oral sex, both from his wife and his boyfriend.
Read Gerald Clarke's Garland bio for the juicy details.
— magazine editor **ED MARGULIES**

✳

Everyone always points out the Neely O'Hara character in *Valley
of the Dolls* is based on Judy Garland. They never say her so-called
fag husband Ted Casablanca is based on Vincente Minnelli.
— book reviewer **DAVE REYNOLDS**

✳

Someone once said the perfect marriage would be
between a blind wife and a deaf husband.
— comedian **GREG GIRALDO**

✳

After they circumcised David, they threw out the wrong bit.
— **IRENE MAYER SELZNICK**, daughter of
MGM's Louis B. Mayer, on ex-husband David O.
Selznick, producer of *Gone with the Wind*

I won't name famous names—you'll read my upcoming book—but he's a prick, and she's a bitch, so it was really considerate of them to marry each other, making only two people unhappy instead of four.

— talk-show host **SKIP E. LOWE**

✳

I begged [game-show producers] Goodson-Todman to hire my wife, to get her out of my what little hair I had left. . . . If she hadn't become a *Match Game* regular and I wasn't busy working, our marriage would have been X-amount shorter.

— **JACK KLUGMAN** on ex Brett Somers

✳

I love Mickey Mouse more than any woman I've ever known.

— husband and father of two daughters **WALT DISNEY**

✳

Sandra [Dee] might have the bigger career, . . . but mine is more important because I'm the husband.

— singer **BOBBY DARIN**

✳

Beat a woman with a hammer, and you'll make gold.

— **RUSSIAN PROVERB**

✳

I like girls, not women. Wives are women. They're not much fun.

— **DEAN MARTIN**

✳

Divorce is a bitch. Like half the people who do it.

— shock-comedian **SAM KINISON**

Divorce means never having to say you're sorry again.
— **RYAN O'NEAL** (*Love Story*)

✳

I caught the flu once, but I didn't have to keep it.
— **MARTY FELDMAN**, on why he favored divorce

✳

I suppose so. Hope springs infernal.
— **GROUCHO MARX**, when asked if he
would consider marrying again

✳

One of my two husbands was a book publisher, Michael Joseph.
When we divorced, he asked whether I wanted the children,
and I said no, he was welcome to them. But I did want my cat.
— UK actress **HERMIONE GINGOLD**, author
of *How to Grow Old Disgracefully*

✳

I briefly married a man I wasn't sure I knew and whose
name I forgot several times afterward. That's before I
was diagnosed as bipolar and given medication.
— **PATTY DUKE**

✳

I got married partly in order to learn about sex. I was an idiot.
— **BETTE DAVIS**

I married my first husband [barber Frank White] because he
smelled so good, my second [gambler Nick Arnstein] because he
looked so good, and my third [producer Billy Rose] because he
thought so good—mostly about the shows he was starring me in.
— **FANNY BRICE**

✳

There's lots of reasons for getting married. . . . Among
the biggest in showbiz is a gay guy covering up.
— hetero actor **KEN BERRY** (*Mayberry R.F.D.*)

✳

Gay people have the same right to lose
half their stuff as everyone else.
— hetero comic **RICHARD JENI**

✳

If they're both stars, a gay and a lesbian have the
same enemy—the truth—and neither can blackmail
the other. That's a practical marriage!
— Hollywood publicist **RONNIE CHASEN**

✳

David Bowie met his future wife because she
and he were dating the same chap.
— UK writer **GIL GIBSON**

His agent engaged him to his lesbian secretary. Soon the
marriage ended, Rock left the agent, and she blackmailed
Rock for the rest of his life. . . . After he died, she profited
further with a book, My *Husband Rock Hudson*. Then she
died, still pretending she'd been in love with Rock.

— Oscar-winning actress **CLAIRE TREVOR**, a friend of Hudson

We have our ups and downs, but Brynn is
a wonderful, devoted mother.

— **PHIL HARTMAN**, whom Brynn shot dead in 1998 before
shooting herself, thus orphaning their two small children

Playwright **GEORGE S. KAUFMAN:** I like your bald
head, Marc. It feels just like my wife's behind.

Playwright **MARC CONNOLLY:** So it does, George.

They say third time's the charm.

— **TOM NEAL**, star of the cult movie *Detour*, who
fatally shot his third wife. Sentenced to 10 years in
jail, he died in 1972, 8 months after his release.

I counted eight.

— **BONNY LEE BAKLEY**, murdered wife of actor Robert
Blake, on the number of her pre-Blake marriages; when a
reporter told her at least one more marriage was documented
in the county recorder's office in Bakley's hometown of
Memphis, Tennessee, she added, "Oh, nine, then."

The cat is a woman with fur and all her bad
qualities, . . . a being to shun and even fear.
— ailurophobic writer **NORMAN MAILER**,
who stabbed one of his several wives

✳

Fancy that Napoleon, who tried to conquer all of Europe, was
afraid of cats, . . . screamed when one entered his tent in Egypt. . . .
His biggest regret in life was ending his first marriage to Josephine,
whom he loved the most, because she didn't yield him an heir.
— historian Dr. **WILBUR JACOBS**

✳

Since our breakup, I have been required to live in an
environment in which Elizabeth would never reside.
— construction worker **LARRY FORTENSKY**
after Elizabeth Taylor divorced him

✳

My sister married a backwoods guy. The morning she fixed
their first breakfast, she asked, "Honey, how would you
like your eggs cooked?" He said, "Hey, that'd be great!"
— comedienne **SAKYA STRINGER**

✳

People envy me. . . . Yes, the sex was great. But
then comes the rest of the relationship.
— eight-times-wed musician **ARTIE SHAW**, whose
wives included Lana Turner and Ava Gardner

The worst thing a spouse can tell you is whatever
follows "I'm only telling you this for your own good"
or "I'm only saying this because I love you."
— *Playboy* publisher **HUGH HEFNER**

✳

She's like that old joke about Philadelphia. First
prize, four years with Joan. Second prize, eight.
— ex-husband **FRANCHOT TONE** on Joan Crawford

✳

Good advice, ladies: Don't surprise your husband by coming
home early one day and bursting into the bedroom. He might
have somebody else in there. It could even be a man. This has
happened to at least a handful of major actresses. *Call ahead.*
— Detroit columnist **SHIRLEY EDER**

✳

Gracie comes home one day, loaded down with flowers. . . .
I ask where she's been and why all the flowers? She says,
"George, dear, your mind is slipping. This morning you said
I should visit Marge in the hospital and take her flowers."
— **GEORGE BURNS** on wife Gracie Allen

✳

My husband will never chase another woman.
He's too fine, too decent, too old.
— **GRACIE ALLEN** on George Burns

If you marry an older man and stay together, eventually
you'll have to become his nurse or hire one.
— talk-show host **VIRGINIA GRAHAM**

✳

It's a matter of opinion.
— UK actress **HERMIONE GINGOLD**, when
asked if her ex-husband was still living

✳

I never married because there was no need. I have three pets
at home, which answer the same purpose as a husband. I have
a dog which growls every morning, a parrot which swears
all afternoon, and a cat that comes home late at night.
— British novelist **MARIE CORELLI**

✳

Some women do look for father figures. . . . I don't think
very many men out there are looking for mother figures.
— **MADELINE KAHN**

✳

When my father, for a very special anniversary,
gave my mother a small piece of cheap costume
jewelry, she gave him a big piece of her mind.
— **MARIA CALLAS**

✳

Anniversaries are numbers, and unfortunately a lot of long-lived
marriages are endurance tests. A marriage should last as long
as it remains mutually happy. Quality first; quantity big deal.
— **BEA ARTHUR**

We started as husband and wife, but it
ended like brother and sister.

— **ELIZABETH TAYLOR** on older British actor Michael Wilding

✳

In Tinseltown more men are concerned with the
loss of their hair than the loss of a wife. Makes
sense: Hair is very difficult to replace.

— **TED BESSELL** (*That Girl*)

✳

You can often tell a gay celebrity marriage if they've been
together a really long time. Most straight male celebs
keep exchanging the wife for a younger model. . . . Long-
term marriages are sometimes about friendship rather than
sex, like, say, Jack Benny or Danny Kaye. . . . Sometimes
such marriages adopt, usually a girl, to blend in.

— Hollywood casting director **BARBARA DODD REMSEN**

✳

Let's just say, at the services they had to sedate Ranger Bob.

— *Hollywood Squares'* **PAUL LYNDE**, answering, "Did the
recently deceased Smokey the Bear leave a widow?"

✳

You take each other for better or for worse, but
you shouldn't take each other for granted.

— **LUCILLE BALL**

✳

Immature love says, "I love you because I need you."
Mature love says, "I need you because I love you."

— psychologist **ERICH FROMM**

6

Personal Life

Dress me slowly, I'm in a hurry.

— **NAPOLEON BONAPARTE**, reportedly, to his valet

✳

Mr. Harris, your fly is open.

— playwright **GEORGE S. KAUFMAN**, on visiting the office of
theater producer Jed Harris, who received him completely nude

✳

My husband . . . doesn't like my picking out his
clothes. But he likes to pick out mine.

— **CAROLYN BESSETTE KENNEDY**, who died
along with her husband, John F. Kennedy Jr., when
a private plane he was piloting crashed

✳

I do not like them. . . . I'm afraid I overreacted when my wife first
wore one. You see, for my generation, it's quite a shocking look.

— **CARY GRANT** on the miniskirt. His wife
later said he hit her for wearing one.

✳

I keep my campaign promises, but I never
promised to wear stockings.

— Connecticut governor **ELLA GRASSO**

✳

Ladies, avoid going to a party in a dress that makes you
look like you're going to get up and sing after dinner.

— movie-costume designer **EDITH HEAD**

I learned never to wear a necklace whose beads are bigger than some of your facial features. That necklace was all anyone mentioned after seeing me in *Annie Hall*.

— **JANET MARGOLIN**

✳

The jean is the destructor! It is a dictator! It is destroying creativity. The jean must be stopped!

— French fashion designer **PIERRE CARDIN**

✳

Frilly, silly skirts, feathers, and ruffles are something I wouldn't wear in real life. For the screen, I usually avoid them like the plague.

— **BARBARA STANWYCK**

✳

Kate wore a skirt [off-screen] only once, to my knowledge. We were going to a funeral, and I insisted I wouldn't take her if she wore her eternal pants.

— **GEORGE CUKOR**, who directed Katharine Hepburn 10 times

✳

Joan Crawford believed dressing up when you go out is simply good manners. Okay, but she overdid on her wardrobe. She even had a special outfit for answering fan mail.

— costar **JACK PALANCE**

✳

Explain this, but give me a valid reason: Why should a woman paint a difference face over her own? Men don't.

— actress-turned-publicist **PATTY DWORKIN**

In real life I'm allergic to gadgets. They just don't work for me, not even those plastic cards for hotel room doors.
— **DESMOND LLEWELYN**, James Bond's gadget-master Q, who died at 85 in a car crash, returning home alone from a book signing

✳

People think California's so liberal, but they've had right-wing nuts a-plenty. One pro-NRA state senator publicly warned that microwave ovens can be more dangerous than guns.
— comedian **DUSTIN DIAMOND**

✳

Just think—guns have a constitutional amendment protecting them, and women don't.
— **ELEANOR SMEAL** in a fundraising letter for the Fund for the Feminist Majority

✳

Let's be objective about this. Guns are not the real problem. The real problem is bullets.
— comedian **PAT PAULSEN**

✳

Silence is golden. Unless you have children. Then it's ominous.
— humorist **ERMA BOMBECK**

✳

After I grew up, the first time I answered the doorbell and heard the loud words "Trick or treat!" on Halloween, it sounded like a threat.
— comedian **MIKE DESTEFANO**

Children today are tyrants. They contradict their parents,
gobble their food, and tyrannize their teachers.
— **SOCRATES**

✳

I could now afford all the things I couldn't
have as a kid, if only I didn't have kids.
— comedienne **PHYLLIS DILLER**

✳

Fun for the whole family? No such thing. Manufacturers and
amusement parks made it up. "Fun for the whole family" is
bound to be excruciating for one or more family members.
— singer **MEL TORMÉ**

✳

You can travel first class, or you can bring the children. For me,
first travel and enjoy your life, then have children, if at all.
— actress **ARLENE GOLONKA** (*The Andy Griffith Show*)

✳

I remember when *outing* meant a family picnic.
— comedian **RODNEY DANGERFIELD**

✳

A straight friend innocently asked if I like to camp?
I said, "Well, sometimes but not in public."
— gay comedian **FRANK MAYA**

✳

God or Frank Lloyd Wright or somebody created motels
so we wouldn't have to go camping anymore.
— comedian **ANNE MEARA**

I like to help create products that are useful
around the home, especially the kitchen, because
that's where food and water come out of.

— **FARRAH FAWCETT**, who plugged Farrah posters, Farrah
dolls, Farrah wigs, and a Farrah Fawcett (faucet) plumbing fixture

✳

It wasn't very flattering, but it was a job. . . . I did an ad for, I think,
Wella shampoo where Farrah Fawcett was the girl with pretty hair.
They hired me for the one with ugly hair. And I have good hair!

— **PENNY MARSHALL**, the first woman to direct two
movies that grossed more than $100 million each

✳

I have very often deprived myself of the necessities of
life, but I have never consented to give up a luxury.

— French author **COLETTE**

✳

I never drink coffee at lunch. I find it keeps
me awake for the afternoon.

— attributed to **RONALD REAGAN**

✳

It's ironic and deliberate that you can buy cigarettes near any
supermarket or drugstore entrance, but you have to hobble
all the way to the back to get medical prescriptions.

— Oscar-winner **EILEEN HECKART**

✳

If you don't mind smelling like a peanut for two or three
days, peanut butter is darn good shaving cream.

— Senator **BARRY GOLDWATER**

I didn't know what to get my nephew for his 15th birthday, so I asked him, "What you want for your birthday?" He said, "I want a watch." So I let him!
— comedienne **JACKIE "MOMS" MABLEY**

✳

If blind people wear sunglasses, why don't deaf people wear earmuffs?
— comedian **NORM MACDONALD**

✳

My husband Fang's not a thinker. Doesn't read books and hardly reads menus. He thinks paparazzi is a pizza topping.
— PHYLLIS DILLER

✳

If at first you don't succeed, order pizza.
— novelist **JACKIE COLLINS**

✳

How could we, not so long ago, have been so stupid to believe that man-made, chemical, corporate margarine was healthy but nature-made butter was not? The oleo industry spent millions duping millions of us. . . . With logic and actual facts replacing advertising, we got unduped.
— actor **KEN BERRY** (*Mama's Family*)

Unlike Betty Crocker, Duncan Hines was real, . . . a culinary
critic, before the eponymous cake mixes. . . . He made enemies,
calling southern cooking greasy and telling readers that
restaurants advertising "homemade cooking" were phony.
He alienated farmers who claimed their pricey pigs were
peanut-fed, pointing out that if pigs lived on peanuts,
they'd be inedible because their flesh would be too oily.
— nutritionist **ADELLE DAVIS**

✳

It's so beautifully arranged on the plate—you know
someone's fingers have been all over it.
— **JULIA CHILD**

✳

Think about this seriously before you answer: Would
you like a scoop of ice cream in your coffee?
— **LEONARD COHEN**, Canadian writer and singer/songwriter

✳

Funny how croutons always come in airtight packages
even though they're basically stale bread.
— **LOUIE ANDERSON**

✳

When Marilyn Monroe was dating Jewish playwright Arthur
Miller, his family served them chicken soup with matzo balls
three nights in a row. Marilyn supposedly asked Arthur,
"Isn't there any other part of a matzo that people eat?"
— columnist **BOYD MCDONALD**

Now that Marilyn Monroe has converted to
Judaism, Arthur Miller can eat her.
— a kosher but double-meaning quip that got
OSCAR LEVANT taken off the air on live TV in 1958

✳

Animal-rights activists are sometimes labeled extremists. I
think it's extreme to eat an animal more than once a day.
— **GRAYSON HALL** (*Dark Shadows*)

✳

If animals could talk to us, we'd all be vegetarians.
— **DORIS DAY**

✳

Daily Special: Hare Pie—$1.75
For the Kiddies: Bunny on a Bun—$.75
— **MENU** at a Springdale, Nevada, inn

✳

Meat is a euphemism that lets us ignore where the flesh
comes from and how. To eat it is a choice, but at least give
a thought to the animal that died for your enjoyment.
— director **AGNES VARDA**

✳

Fox hunting is the unspeakable in pursuit of the inedible.
— **OSCAR WILDE**

✳

In the end, what is dieting? All that extra effort just to
earn five more years in an assisted-living facility.
— actor **JOHN CANDY**

I've decided to live to be 100.

— publisher and fitness authority **J. I. RODALE**, on Dick Cavett's talk show, during which the 72-year-old suffered a fatal heart attack (the episode didn't air)

✳

I don't have many goals left. . . . One is to reach 100. I'd like that.

— stage, film, and TV star **EDDIE ALBERT** (*Green Acres*), who lived to 99. His son died the following year at 55.

✳

Dying is not a problem if you can do it alone. Yet people say, "How sad, he died alone." Who wants to have to die and be polite at the same time?

— author **QUENTIN CRISP**

✳

I met Kirk Douglas not long after he turned 100. He looked very lifelike.

— TV host **BOB SAGET**

✳

Seeing Elvis at the end was sad, . . . chubby-faced, pot-bellied, pants bursting at the seams, . . . his whole attitude sloppily unprofessional. Either diet or retire. You're getting paid, and customers don't want their fantasies shattered.

— Broadway talent agent **BEVERLY ANDERSON TRAUBE**

✳

Definition of an anorexic: somebody who went on a diet and never came back.

— screenwriter **DOROTHY KINGSLEY**

Where do you go to, uh, get some of this anorexia?
— overweight actress (and winner of two Oscars)
SHELLEY WINTERS on *The Tonight Show*

✳

The gourmet had a royal feast.
— ghost writer **COLINOT BONNARD**, referencing William
Buckland, who in 1848 ate the heart of Louis XIV. It was traditional
to embalm a king's heart, but after the French Revolution in 1789,
several were stolen. That of the "Sun King," who died in 1715,
wound up in England, where Buckland, who'd vowed to sample
every existing animal, extended his diet to a royal human.

✳

Two cannibals eating a clown. One says to the
other, "Does this taste funny to you?"
— comedian/magician **TOMMY COOPER**

✳

I believe that if ever I had to practice cannibalism, I
might manage if there were enough tarragon around.
— chef **JAMES BEARD**

✳

If someone was hurt by what I said [in her comedy routine], I'd
say, "Stop eating, okay? Pull away from the table!" I'd like to sit
around like a house all day and inhale doughnuts, but come on!
Have a little respect for yourself. Use a little self-control. Pull
away from the table and say, "I'm done." How hard is that?
I'd say, "I'm offended by the fact that you're a house
when you should be a person, okay? So we're even!"
— **JUDY TENUTA**

Never eat more than you can lift.

— MISS PIGGY

My favorite sandwich is peanut butter, bologna,
cheddar cheese, lettuce, and mayonnaise on
toasted bread with lots of catsup on the side.

— 1968 presidential candidate **HUBERT
HUMPHREY**. Winning candidate Richard Nixon
likewise considered ketchup a vegetable.

The year before he died, Elvis Presley flew to Denver in his private
jet to eat an 8,000-calorie sandwich made out of a hollowed-
out bread loaf stuffed with a jar of peanut butter, a jar of jelly,
and a pound of bacon. Then flew right back to Memphis.

— biographer **ALBERT GOLDMAN**

His doctor told Marlon Brando, when he was gaining so much
weight, that he had to control his habits. Like no more candle-
lit dinners for two, unless there was one other person.

— comedian **JERRY STILLER** (Ben's father)

I'm at the age when food has taken the place of sex in my life.
In fact, I've just had a mirror put over my kitchen table.

— RODNEY DANGERFIELD

Fat people used to be vaguely embarrassed. Nowadays they
get angry! They're not a legitimate minority. . . . It's an
unhealthy choice, not to mention unattractive. I was making
a health-conscious statement. . . . Afterward, I had to choose
between an apology and possibly losing my livelihood!

— CLORIS LEACHMAN

It is not fatness. It is development.

— ex-sex symbol **ANITA EKBERG** on her excess poundage

Isn't it a form of child abuse when parents raise fat children?

— MARY TYLER MOORE

I like pop-up toaster tarts for breakfast. But if I'm in
a hurry I prefer those little purse-shaped fruit pies.
Unlike the tarts, they don't need any cooking.

— comedian **KEVIN BARNETT**

I was having Rice Krispies for breakfast. . . . The cat
balanced on my thigh and peered into my bowl . . . stared
into it. "Want a nice bowl of Mice Krispies?" The cat
ignored my joke, and it dawned on me she wanted to know
who was in the bowl going, "Snap, crackle, pop."

— actor **PHILIP SEYMOUR HOFFMAN**

I lost 20 pounds one time. . . . I asked the doctors
where it went, but nobody knows.

— **SHELLEY WINTERS**. Lost weight reportedly converts
mostly to carbon dioxide and is breathed out.

✳

Nature will castigate those who don't masticate.

— early health nut **HORACE FLETCHER** (1849–
1919), the "Great Masticator," who advocated
chewing each morsel of food 32 times

✳

There are cyanide compounds in the seeds of apples,
apricots, plums, and cherries. They aren't harmful
except in excess. One man ate a cup of apple seeds he'd
collected. He died quickly—cyanide kills fast.

— Canadian scientist **KEN MONEY**

✳

Some information is completely irrelevant. Like the
expiration dates on things like cookies or a tin of fudge.

— radio host **CONNIE NORMAN**

✳

No man is lonely while eating spaghetti.

— Sir **ROBERT MORLEY**

✳

Loathe fat people? . . . I certainly don't admire them.
They're digging their graves with their own teeth. I think
to be terribly overweight is incredibly unhealthy.

— **JOAN COLLINS**

I hate fiction-loving, greedy food companies that sell
"gluten-free" products that never included gluten to
begin with and as if it's more healthy. A small percentage
of people have problems with gluten. Most people
have been eating gluten regularly for millennia.

— health writer **FRANKIE LINDER**

✳

I recently began eating more for nutrition than low calories.
I cared too much what men think of my looks . . . and wore
high heels, which are damaging over the long run, to please
them. But really, how much do *they* sacrifice to look good
for *us?* Anything? It's tit for tat, honey, or forget *it!*

— singer **NANCY WILSON**

✳

Women spend an inordinate amount of time caring
what men think about them. Most women would be
surprised how seldom men really think about them.

— **BETTY BERZON**, psychotherapist

✳

Women spend more time wondering what men are
thinking than men actually spend thinking.

— comedian **SHIRLEY HEMPHILL**

✳

Men use more words than women. They like to think they're
expressing themselves. But women have more thoughts.

— **BARBARA WALTERS**

Psychoanalysis is faster for men than for women because when it's time to revert to their childhood, men are halfway there.
— Dr. **ANNA FREUD** (Sigmund's daughter)

My psychiatrist once said to me, "Maybe life isn't for everyone."
— actor/pianist **OSCAR LEVANT**

My choice for the best psychiatrist is a puppy licking your face.
— **CINDY WILLIAMS**

Gray matter, which comprises the brain's outer layer, generally shrinks with age. However, it can grow with exercise, learning, and meditation. . . . It further shrinks in regards to obesity, smoking, and diabetes.
— Sir **ROGER BANNISTER**, medical doctor and the first person to run a mile in under four minutes

Society minimizes the seriousness of nonvisible illnesses. . . . But mental illness, particularly depression, is more widespread than people realize. It's the leading cause of suicide.
— singer **NAOMI JUDD**, who took her own life in 2022

To my friends' amazement, I did not kill Brett Somers, who
burned down my house. Accidentally, I must add, but thanks
to laziness and uncounted martinis. . . . Since I couldn't afford
central heating, I had old-fashioned individual floor heaters. My
houseguest Brett turned one on to 95 degrees. In another room,
she was guzzling away, listening to records, and talking to my dog
Bingo. She didn't notice that flames were engulfing my house.
My son and I had gone to the movies. Brett preferred to stay in
and drink. So when we returned, my beautiful house . . . was
gone. With everything in it. Except Brett and my dear Bingo.

— MARCIA WALLACE

There is so much upkeep with a house, but the
truth is, you can get your husband to do most chores
if you suggest maybe he's too old to do it.

— KATHERINE HELMOND (*Who's the Boss?*)

I told my mother [Debbie Reynolds] once that
I really hate being middle-aged. She smiled and
said, "Don't worry, dear, you'll outgrow it."

— CARRIE FISHER

For too much of my life, my father scared me. He
comes on very strong. . . . You don't want to see him
mad. . . . I've brought him a lot of bad publicity, not
purposely. But it has helped even up the score.

— ERIC DOUGLAS, youngest of Kirk's four sons

My father abandoned my mother, Ruthie, and her two daughters. That was not then uncommon, and men weren't penalized. By law, there were no deadbeat fathers. But it made my mother strong, and it made me strong. It didn't do much for my sister Barbara.
— **BETTE DAVIS**. Joan Crawford's father also abandoned his wife and children.

If a mother wants to attach a baby to her boob, do one side, then the other side, burp him, get him to take a nap, then do it all over again, go right ahead. For me, it just wasn't possible.
— devoted mom **IVANA TRUMP**

What if you have a daughter, and she is prettier than you? Or she is ugly?
— **GINA LOLLOBRIGIDA**, who had a son

Natalie Wood's mom was so desperate to have and manage a star-daughter, . . . she even acted as a pimp toward Natalie. She sent her, in her midteens, into the lion's den more than once, . . . including a rape by Kirk Douglas that has hardly seen the light of print.
— friend and costar **TAB HUNTER** to TV interviewer Carl David

If I had a kid who got a tattoo, I'd plotz—and I'm not even Jewish. . . . Clones like to get tattoos. Nonindividuals realize they're undistinctive, so they decorate themselves individually.
— **ROSE MARIE** (*The Dick Van Dyke Show*)

Girls, think of the long-term. Say you get a tattoo of a butterfly.
. . . By the time you're 50, it might resemble a condor.
— PHYLLIS DILLER

※

Nature gives you the face you have when you are
20. Life shapes the face you have at 30. But it is
up to you to earn the face you have at 50.
— GABRIELLE "COCO" CHANEL

※

Start every day off with a smile, and get it over with.
— W. C. FIELDS

※

Good manners are the extra effort we
make towards people we dislike.
— QUENTIN CRISP

※

I'm a Jewish Buddhist or Buddhist Jew, . . . and most religions
say to love your enemies. It's more honestly realistic to say,
"Just treat your friends and everyone you meet a little better."
— Canadian musician and writer **LEONARD COHEN**

During my school days, if someone was asked what his
mother did, he'd invariably say, "She's just a housewife." . . .
It may be humorous to say "domestic engineer," but where's
the harm? Without housewives, the world would stop.
— ED ASNER

You have to be sensitive to people different from yourself. That's why "politically correct" began. Like using neutral words instead of insulting ones for minorities. . . . Anything can be taken too far, but being politically correct is still a good concept and increasingly required.

— actress and heiress **DINA MERRILL**

He was needlessly rude and I suppose insecure. [Frank Sinatra] knew I was a comedienne, so when we met and I said, 'Eh, *paisan*," I was referring to our shared Italian heritage. Instead, he cold-shouldered me and gruffly said, "I'm an American." Well, what did he think *I* was, Swahili?

— **KAYE BALLARD**

Not a role model, . . . [but] he was proclaimed an American hero after declaring he'd shot 4,280 buffalo. He made a living showing up as "Buffalo Bill." The phrase *endangered species* wasn't in the 19th-century vocabulary.

— UCSB professor **FELIPE POWELL**

There are shockingly few laws to punish those who torture or kill animals, including dogs and cats. Please get involved and help change this.

— Hollywood's number-1 box-office actress, founder of the **DORIS DAY** Animal Foundation (ddaf.org)

If nothing else works, chop their heads off!
— **MUHAMMAD ALI**, paid anticockroach spokesman.
Cockroaches' heads don't bleed and aren't needed
to breathe. They only use their heads to eat. A headless
cockroach takes time to die—from starvation.

A male friend asked a cat expert I recommended if
getting neutered would make his cat happier. She said
it definitely would. There'd be less catting around and
more sticking close to home. She meant the man.
— cat lover **SANDY DENNIS**

A house without a cat or dog in it is not a home.
— character actress **KATHLEEN FREEMAN**

The Academy rule was no alcohol served backstage during the
Oscars. Actors, even stars, tend awfully towards alcoholism. Well,
Peter O'Toole had been nominated several times but, amongst
several other highly gifted non-Americans, never won. On the
other hand, such Yanks as James Stewart and John Wayne had.
In order for O'Toole to show up and receive his well-deserved
honorary Oscar, the Academy had to temporarily break its rule.
— UK actress **GERALDINE MCEWAN**

I'm afraid my costar [in *Sibling Rivalry*] was a classic
alcoholic, always up at the crack of ice. I'm not being
facetious, . . . and it's not mean if it's true.
— **KIRSTIE ALLEY** on Carrie Fisher

I know ladies who say they don't get tipsy.

No, they get overserved.

— **ROGER MOORE**

When alcoholics are made public, many seek publicity to
pretend it's over and they're on the wagon and keeping fit.
Like Truman Capote. He did a magazine photo session during
which he kept guzzling off-camera. When it came time to
pose on a stationary bike, two assistants had to help him get
up and mount it. . . . Tru was so soused, he nearly fell off.

— showbiz author **DAVID SHIPMAN**

I ask myself if there are more or fewer hard drinkers than
in the past? Liquor has an anesthetizing effect, and we still
live in difficult times, . . . with problems that never before
existed. Analyze them, and realize that much or most of
this mess has arrived from human overpopulation.

— Portuguese director **MANOEL DE
OLIVEIRA**, who lived to 106

Not before anesthesia was invented.

— historical novelist **GORE VIDAL**, when asked which
period of history he'd have chosen to live in

7

Pretentious or Stupid?

CHAD: Lately, Dave, you act as if you don't like me anymore.

DAVE: No, it's just that you've gotten so pretentious lately.

CHAD: Pretentious? *Moi?*

＊

I did not use paint. I made myself up morally.

— legendary Italian actress **ELEANORA DUSE**

＊

I try to be Godlike.

— MICHAEL JACKSON

＊

God is really another artist like me. I am God.

— PABLO PICASSO

＊

I don't claim to have invented sex, but I've
certainly helped the country rediscover it.

— 1930s sex symbol **MAE WEST**,
whose movies led to stricter censorship

＊

I never claimed to have invented the motion
picture, but I did do more than my share, yes.

— actress/producer **MARY PICKFORD**, cofounder
of United Artists. The star, who as an adult played
little girls, claimed, "Putting sound to movies would
be like putting lipstick on the *Venus de Milo*."

I have discovered the dance. I have discovered
the art which has been lost for 2,000 years.
— **ISADORA DUNCAN**

✳

My only regret in the theater is that I could
never sit out front and watch me.
— **JOHN BARRYMORE**, nicknamed "The Great Profile"

✳

I was at first rather surprised that anyone
chose to play [Joan of Arc] after I did.
— Dame **SYBIL THORNDIKE**, highly
acclaimed in Shaw's play *Saint Joan*

✳

I did more for James Bond [in *Thunderball*, 1965] than James Bond
did for me. The picture was an enormous success, but later roles
were not up to my standard or ability. . . . And remember that
it was I who killed the villain and I saved James Bond's life.
— French actress **CLAUDINE AUGER**

✳

I admire Leonard Bernstein but not as much as he does.
He uses music as an accompaniment to his conducting.
— pianist, composer, and wit **OSCAR LEVANT**

✳

I was very ill and afraid for my sanity, but
that was before I changed my name.
— **PRINCE** (the "artist formerly known as")

I avoid hearing other composers' material. That way, I won't
copy them. Even unconsciously. Or subconsciously.
— composer **RUDOLF FRIML** at 90 in 1969

✳

I only read my own books.
— **BARBARA CARTLAND**, nondiabetic

✳

We sent out a young woman to interview Barbara
Cartland. One of the first things she told her, rather
imperiously, was that she'd published over 100 novels.
Our reporter said, "Oh. One for every year?"
— **BRITISH *PHOTOPLAY* EDITOR**

✳

They say I've made hairspray acceptable for men. I
don't know about that, but I am proud of my hair.
— **JACK LORD** (*Hawaii Five-O*)

✳

I knew Rock Hudson was gay after we met
and he did not fall in love with me.
— **GINA LOLLOBRIGIDA**, on her costar

Ignorance was rife then. I would get asked, "Are there gay Chinese? Gay Hispanics?" There are gay *everything*! Recently someone said, "But there aren't gay terrorists." I said, "Ever hear of the PLO's Yassir Arafat?" He was being outed, so he married his secretary and had a daughter. But he continued with his real private life.

— writer/activist **LARRY KRAMER** to *Village Voice* columnist Boyd McDonald

✳

Slump? I ain't in no slump. I just ain't hittin.'

— baseball power hitter **YOGI BERRA**

✳

I fired him because he wouldn't respect the authority of the president. I didn't fire him because he was a dumb son of a bitch, although he was, but that's not against the law for generals. If it was, half to three-quarters of them would be in jail.

— **HARRY S. TRUMAN**

✳

Which is what? What the fuck is it? I am one, you know. And if there isn't, I don't care.

— **JOHN LENNON**, when asked if he believed in genius

✳

I feel I'm an aristocrat in my field of endeavor. My being part of *Bonanza* was like Isaac Stern sitting in with Lawrence Welk.

— **PERNELL ROBERTS**, who played the eldest Cartwright son and departed the show due to "bland and trivial scripts"

We have mastered the mystical talent of speaking
to the big cats. They are our family and would never
attack us. . . . We communicate from the heart.
— Siegfried and Roy's **SIEGFRIED FISCHBACHER**
before a tiger put Roy in a wheelchair

✳

We can fly, you know. We just don't know how to think
the right thoughts and levitate ourselves off the ground.
— **MICHAEL JACKSON**

✳

Michael Jackson's album was only called *Bad* because
there wasn't enough room on the sleeve for *Pathetic*.
— rival **PRINCE**

✳

I believe in white supremacy until the blacks are educated to a
point of responsibility. I don't believe in giving authority and
positions of leadership and judgment to irresponsible people.
— **JOHN WAYNE** in a 1971 *Playboy* interview

✳

Facts are stupid things—stubborn things, I should say.
— **RONALD REAGAN**, addressing the
Republican National Convention in 1988

✳

Members of the Public Committing Suicide from
This Tower Do So at Their Own Risk
— **SIGN ON LORD BERNERS'S ENGLISH ESTATE**,
where he housed white doves dyed in several
colors and in 1935 built a 141-foot-high tower

Yes. But he was only an emperor.

— stage legend **SARAH BERNHARDT**, replying to an American who noted that her US visit was receiving more publicity than the recent one of Dom Pedro of Brazil

✳

I can't remember a day in my life when I wasn't famous.

— child star and adult superstar **ELIZABETH TAYLOR**

✳

Imagine, darling, having all of Hollywood at your foot!

— UK actress **CORAL BROWNE**, upon seeing gossip columnist Radie Harris (who had only one leg) at a party, enthroned above a gaggle of young actors seated on the floor

✳

I could play her better than that.

— **JULIE HARRIS** to an actor while waiting in line at the Kennedy Center in Washington, DC, to be presented to Queen Elizabeth II

✳

Go away, little girl. I don't need you anymore.

— **JOAN CRAWFORD** to a fan after marrying Pepsi-Cola bigwig Alfred Steele and intending to retire from acting

✳

Do I *need* this?

— **KIRK DOUGLAS**'s reaction when a young girl asked for his autograph

Having recognized my budding genius at an early age, [my mother] took me to a children's audition at a theater where I did my little act and got hired immediately. The stage manager . . . said to her, "Shall we say three pounds a week?" and my mother replied, "I'm sorry, but we couldn't possibly afford to pay that much."

— **NOËL COWARD**

✳

My doctor told me I have the heart of a 20-year-old. I told him, "Doctor, you should not have peeked into my laboratory."

— horror-movie star **BORIS KARLOFF**

✳

I have the skin of a 26-year-old.

— **MAE WEST**, in her 70s. A 26-year-old what?

✳

Any girl can look glamorous. All she has to do is stand still and look stupid.

— **HEDY LAMARR**, secretly Jewish actress from Austria sometimes described as the most beautiful movie star ever

✳

I don't think President Bush is doing anything at all about AIDS. In fact, I'm not even sure he knows how to spell AIDS.

— **ELIZABETH TAYLOR** on Ronald Reagan's successor

✳

The word *like* has become a virus in our language. . . . Yesterday I heard a young woman on her cell phone say, "Okay, then. I'll meet you, like, at exactly four o'clock." Wasn't she sure?

— journalist/author **COKIE ROBERTS**

A language is a dialect with an army and navy.

— Russian Jewish linguist **MAX WEINREICH**

✳

No country without an atom bomb could
properly consider itself independent.

— CHARLES DE GAULLE

✳

I have signed legislation today that will outlaw Russia
forever. We begin bombing in five minutes.

— RONALD REAGAN, joking during a microphone
check before starting a radio speech on August 11, 1984

✳

The United States will not be a threat to us for decades.

— ADOLF HITLER in 1940

✳

During World War I, a female singer introduced a song
entitled "She Sits among the Cabbages and Peas." It offended
and embarrassed the Lord Chamberlain [Britain's chief
censor], who banned it. She changed the lyrics to "She Sits
among the Lettuces and Leeks." That satisfied him.

— Sir **JOHN GIELGUD**

✳

[I have] ever looked on Cuba as the most interesting addition
which could ever be made to our system of States.

— imperialist-minded **THOMAS JEFFERSON** in
an 1821 letter to President James Monroe after
the United States won control of Florida

Well, I learned a lot. . . . I went down [to South America]
to find out from them and [learn] their views. You'd
be surprised. They're all individual countries.
— **RONALD REAGAN**

＊

Broadway composer **ALAN JAY LERNER:** Why
do people take an instant dislike to me?
Broadway lyricist **FREDERICK LOEWE:** It saves time.

＊

Katharine Hepburn isn't really standoffish.
She ignores everyone equally.
— former costar **LUCILLE BALL**

＊

I hope I never have need of friends.
— opera diva assoluta **MARIA CALLAS**

＊

What people call insincerity is simply a method
by which we can multiply our personalities.
— **OSCAR WILDE**

＊

Every individual has a given number of heartbeats, and
I don't propose to waste any of mine apologizing.
— contentious Broadway producer **JED HARRIS**

＊

Arrogant, pompous, obnoxious, vain, cruel, verbose, a show-
off. I have been called all of those. Of course, I am.
— sportscaster **HOWARD COSELL**

Sometimes Howard [Cosell] makes me wish
I was a dog and he was a fireplug.

— MUHAMMAD ALI

✳

I am God's gift [to soccer].

— Brazilian soccer champ **PELÉ**

✳

We have to gracefully accept the fact that leading
motion-picture stars are role models for the public.
Where we lead, they typically follow.

— CHARLTON HESTON

✳

Is there no beginning to Charlton Heston's talents? He's
played myriad heroes and nationalities, always with
the same flat American accent and an uncomfortable
expression as if his underwear is too tight.

— British author **ROBIN WOOD**

✳

Chanel has never influenced fashion one bit.

— rival designer **PIERRE CARDIN**. Of course she
did, but rival designer Elsa Schiaparelli observed, "That
damn bitch sold the same jacket for 35 years!"

✳

Chanel was a big success, a rare woman with a financial empire.
But a small person. Selfish, bitchy, and her politics were atrocious.
She was pro-Nazi. After the war she clammed up about that.

— LAUREN BACALL. There is recent evidence
that Chanel may have been a Nazi spy.

Hollywood has a stupid and pernicious habit of casting blond actors as Nazis. Look at photos of the leading Nazis. . . . How many were blond? . . . According to Hollywood, all Jews are brown-eyed. Look around, dummies. Most Jews I've seen have blue eyes, not just Paul Newman and Barbra Streisand.

— author **ALEXANDER DOTY**

✳

Audrey Hepburn was estranged from her British father but close to her Dutch mother. Unfortunately, the woman was loud and self-righteous, and after Audrey became a global icon, it took significant whitewashing and covering up to hide the fact that the woman had been cheerfully, openly pro-Hitler.

— biographer **C. DAVID HEYMANN**

✳

I'm not a little girl from a little town making good in a big town. I'm a big girl from a big town making good in a little town.

— 40-ish Brooklynite **MAE WEST**, upon arriving in Hollywood to start her movie career

✳

Princeton is a . . . quaint and ceremonious village of puny demigods on stilts.

— **ALBERT EINSTEIN**, on the university town in which he settled after fleeing Nazi Germany, whose government he'd criticized. J. Edgar Hoover's FBI compiled a massive secret file on Einstein, who criticized anti-Semitism, racism, nationalism, other forms of bigotry, and nuclear bombs.

I don't know where that goofball comedian Gallagher came
from, but somewhere he's depriving a village of its idiot.
— TV host **ROBIN LEACH**

✳

Of course it was embarrassing. My father killed himself.
In a hotel in Times Square. I mean *Times Square*!
— Hollywood super-agent **SUE MENGERS**

✳

I can't do this show. . . . I've never been that poor,
and I've never even *known* a Puerto Rican!
— **STEPHEN SONDHEIM**'s initial reaction when
asked to write the lyrics for *West Side Story*

✳

Talent has long been my predestined path in life.
— singer/actor **MARIO LANZA**

✳

Talent singled me out for the big time.
— **SAMMY DAVIS JR.**

✳

I figured early that I had a musical talent. But if it wasn't
for my parents' show, I'm not sure I'd have got a chance
to show it, . . . to prove it. If I hadn't been their son, then
maybe, possibly I'd have gotten to sing based on my looks.
— **RICK NELSON**, son of TV stars Ozzie and Harriet

Elvis had minimal talent next to somebody like Roy Orbison. But Elvis had that face and the sex appeal. If he'd looked like Roy, he'd be gone and forgotten. Elvis didn't have that much else.
— composer **HARVEY SCHMIDT** (*The Fantasticks*)

＊

In terms of a longer-range career, I see now that I could have used somewhat more personality and somewhat less looks. But what the hell could I have done about it *then*?
— actor **GEORGE NADER**

＊

Zsa Zsa Gabor had three or four operations on her nose, and it got worse every time. It looks like an electric plug that you put in a wall.
— Swedish sex symbol **ANITA EKBERG**

＊

Everyone kept saying I was too pretty, too blonde, too beautiful. But I didn't let that stop me.
— actress **RAINBEAUX SMITH**

＊

Now I look wonderful for my age. Everyone tells me this. It is a relief because up until the late middle age, too many people automatically disliked me. . . . When I walked into a room, heads turned to me and kept looking. I could not help this. Nature gave me that gift. How silly that sometimes I felt guilty for it!
— Mexican actress **DOLORES DEL RÍO**

Women see me and might become borderline nasty. Men aren't much better. The ones who want me but can't have me, . . . the intimidated ones, . . . the ones with wives who don't look like me. . . . It can be a no-win situation.
— **TANYA ROBERTS**, a Charlie's Angel
and a James Bond leading lady

✳

I resent how long it takes people to change their minds that if you look more or less ravishing and with longer hair yet, you must be pretty short on talent.
— UK actress **NATASHA RICHARDSON**

✳

I've always been more talented than I was given credit for in this town. It's not that I want to be the center of attention, but after all these years repeatedly proving myself, why should I share?
— actor-turned-*Family-Feud*-host **RICHARD DAWSON**, who declined to appear on a *TV Guide* cover if it included other game-show hosts

✳

When Al Jolson attends a wedding, he wants to be the bride, and when he attends a funeral he wants to be the corpse.
— writer **LOU ANTHONY**

✳

For a long time, I thought Al was the world's greatest entertainer. Al thought so, too, and I imagine still does.
— Jolson's ex-wife **RUBY KEELER**

With all the due corespect to my fellow [nominees], I
did deserve that award. It was a superb performance!
— Oscar-winner **LILA KEDROVA** (*Zorba the Greek*)

There's probably too much jealousy for me to someday be
presented with an Oscar, know what I mean? Until I'm old, you
know. It's true. . . . But I may have a whole other career ahead
of me as a novelist. Word is out, and it's very encouraging.
— **TONY CURTIS**, whose poorly reviewed first novel was his last

Good career move.
— writer **GORE VIDAL** on rival Truman
Capote's premature death

The book I have completed just might be considered the
second-greatest novel of the 20th century. . . . It certainly
would rank among the top five on any objective critic's list.
— Proust fan **TRUMAN CAPOTE**, who completed
only a few chapters of the tell-all *Answered
Prayers* that lost him most of his friends

They say it might break all records, . . . and, well,
that's something I think I can live with!
— **RONALD REAGAN** on his imminent memoirs, which were
not a big hit. At his editor's insistence, Reagan added mention of
his first wife, whom his second wife had pressured him to omit.

If I'd had to spend my life as an ugly woman, I wouldn't have done it. But I knew I would look good . . . very good. . . . It's sad how many transsexuals do end up looking like men in drag.
— **CHRISTINE JORGENSEN** (born George)

✳

I'm happy and carefree. I'm happy when it's free, and I just don't care. So sue me.
— tightwad comedian **JACK CARTER**

✳

The trouble with unemployment is that the minute you wake up in the morning, you're on the job.
— comedian **SLAPPY WHITE**

✳

Anna Nicole Smith—white trash with money. She took an IQ test. The results were negative.
— **JOAN RIVERS**

✳

If a [sic] adopted child grows up with two gay parents, like two guys or two lesbians, he'll get confused and end up not knowing what sex he is.
— anti-gay activist **DONALD WILDMON**

✳

Gay men who adopt *choose* to be fathers. Surprise and resentment aren't part of it, and they give their offspring time, attention, and encouragement. Also unconditional love—which some straight fathers deny their kid when they find out he's gay.
— Oscar-winning lyricist **HOWARD ASHMAN**

I have a gay relative who with his partner adopted two children. He tells me that for the foreseeable future their sex life seems to be over. Welcome to Planet Parenthood!

— actress **ELIZABETH WILSON** (*9 to 5*)

✳

If you're going to draw attention and get rich being moralistic, how utterly stupid to secretly have extramarital sex or molest underaged girls. Fortunately, a number of these homophobic organizers, preachers, and politicians have gotten caught with their pants and so-called morals down.

— comedian **BOB SMITH**

✳

The best way to discredit Rush Limbaugh is to quote him directly. . . . He is beneath contempt yet commercially viable, a national disgrace. The lies and hateful garbage he spews cannot appeal to anyone with a brain, let alone a heart.

— **GLORIA STEWART** (*Titanic*)

✳

There's verbal violence, and there's physical violence. Both are contemptible, and Don Rickles's "joke" to Frank Sinatra in the audience was asinine: "Make yourself at home, Frank. Hit somebody." *That* is humor?

— Las Vegas costume designer **LLOYD LAMBERT**

Dear Ms. Rivers, . . . If you find it necessary to discuss me, my career, or my kids ever again, I promise you I will get somebody from Chicago to beat your goddamned head off. P.S. You do know that [one's] not allowed to threaten people, so if you go to [the police], show them this letter, they'll arrest me. But I want you to never forget what it said.

— **JERRY LEWIS** to Joan Rivers after she said his telethons were helping his diminished career. Lewis was fired by the Muscular Dystrophy Foundation after many years of Labor Day fundraising telethons. During commercial breaks, he reportedly insulted some of "my kids" in wheelchairs.

Elizabeth wasn't ashamed of her affairs with married and unmarried men or getting fat during the Warner marriage. The one thing that very quietly shamed her was her lack of education. She was never really given one. She wasn't that literate, and her general knowledge was limited. Yet she managed to do an awful lot of good.

— costume designer and Taylor friend **IRENE SHARAFF**

Elizabeth Taylor was overfond of publicity. . . . After John Warner first approached Barbara Walters, he latched onto Liz, and she helped him win his Senate seat. She was a Democrat, semifeminist, progay, but the Republican senator was in for 30 years, consistently voting against women's rights and gay rights. Big boo-boo, Liz.

— publicist **ANDREA JAFFE**

Self-destructive or self-worshiping. . . . This was Jack Lord years before *Hawaii Five-O*. He had a small role in the first Bond movie, *Dr. No*. The character was brought back for the third movie, *Goldfinger*. Lord said he'd do it if he got equal billing with Sean Connery and lots more money. Well, good Lord! Someone else got hired.

— 007 screenwriter **RICHARD MAIBAUM**

✳

Nobody is worth that much, . . . and what's she going to spend it all on, clothes and stuff?

— **JACKIE GLEASON**, after the announcement that Elizabeth Taylor would become the first movie star to earn $1 million for one film (*Cleopatra*)

✳

It's obscene, . . . unheard of. *Why?* What's so special about *her?* . . . And I don't want to listen to a girl deliver the news.

— Los Angeles news anchor **JERRY DUNPHY**, after the announcement that Barbara Walters would become the first million-dollar news anchor

8

Showbiz

If you go on the air with that crap, they're
going to kill you dead in the streets!
— **MICKEY ROONEY** to producer Norman Lear, declining
to star in the pioneering 1970s TV sitcom *All in the Family*

I cannot function in a show that I know is going to go down the
drain only weeks after it airs. . . . Who are you trying to kid?
— **GEORGE PEPPARD** during a reported tantrum. When
he left *Dynasty* he was replaced by John Forsythe.

All the sincerity in Hollywood you can stuff in a flea's navel and
still have room to conceal four caraway seeds and an agent's heart.
— **FRED ALLEN**, radio and TV star

Half the people in Hollywood are dying to be
discovered. The other half are afraid they will be.
— **LIONEL BARRYMORE**

Gossiping is my favorite thing—at the very
least, my second-favorite thing.
— **IVANA TRUMP**

I'd take a juicy bitch at lunch over a guy in bed anytime.
— **JOAN RIVERS**

Everybody wants to be Cary Grant. I want to be Cary Grant.
— **CARY GRANT**

It's only a gilded cage.
— secretly gay or bisexual star **TYRONE POWER**

Natalie Wood was the successful product of a fierce
stage mother who supposedly replied, when the teenager
told her a director had raped her, to keep quiet, since
he was [considering] giving Natalie a *lead*.
— from **THIS AUTHOR**'s *Scandals, Secrets, and Swan Songs*

Acting is the expression of a neurotic impulse. It's a
bum's life. The principal benefit acting has afforded
me is the money to pay for my psychoanalysis.
— MARLON BRANDO

Acting is the most minor of gifts and not a very
high-class way to earn a living. After all, Shirley
Temple could do it at the age of four.
— KATHARINE HEPBURN

Live fast, die young, leave a beautiful corpse.
— motto of **JAMES DEAN**

In Hollywood they'll forgive you if you're two-
faced but not if you're two-chinned.
— actress and union activist **COLLEEN DEWHURST**

As I [get older], . . . I'm beginning to ask, "Is being a movie star at my age worth the trouble?" I don't think it is. . . . It seems I've spent all my life in gyms. I've grown to hate training. I can't go on being a caricature of a he-man. I want simply to be a man and enjoy life as others do.

— **BURT LANCASTER** after performing in *The Swimmer*

✳

Being nominated for an Oscar is like being pregnant with a child someone else may have, for all your labour pains.

— **GLENDA JACKSON**, winner of two
Best Actress Academy Awards

✳

I'm too popular to ever get an Academy Award.
. . . Audiences don't want me highbrow.

— **BURT REYNOLDS**, who turned down the lead in
Coming Home that won another actor an Oscar

✳

A change of pace. I'd like to do something by Noël Coward, . . . [but] they're not going to let me.

— popular actor **JOHN WAYNE**, who did win an Oscar

✳

The Oscars have never been strictly fair, but in general they reflected some good taste. Now it's more about ethnics and racial politics and popularity and block voting and a movie's box office and . . . oh, who cares.

— actor **DEAN STOCKWELL**

He became so popular on TV, they tried to make a movie star out of Liberace. Even a potential Oscar nominee—in his romantic vehicle *Sincerely Yours*, he had not one but *two* leading ladies.

— columnist **LEE GRAHAM**.
The inaccurately titled movie flopped big.

✳

She, or it, is one of the most disgusting "entertainment" creations ever devised.

— **PEGGY LEE**, referring to Miss Piggy. The Muppet was called Miss Piggy Lee until Lee threatened to sue.

✳

It was by no means sure Elvis would make it in movies. He was controversial, many parents detested him, and he appealed far more to girls than boys. He was also hard to place in a conventional musical and had minimal acting talent. But . . . you know what happened. Until he and the so-called Colonel ran his movie career into the ground. Greed and laziness killed their golden goose.

— Presley biographer **ALBERT GOLDMAN**

✳

He won't do drugs. He won't take his pants off without underwear. And he will not be unmanly and let some girl, you know, dominate him.

— **ELVIS PRESLEY**, enumerating what his movie characters would never do

There were complaints because Miss [Tallulah] Bankhead wore
no panties, which was obvious each time the cast climbed up
into the lifeboat—ladies first. . . . Hitch was amused but didn't
wish to interfere, . . . said he didn't know whether "this is a
matter for the costume department, makeup, or hairdressing."

— **HUME CRONYN**, costar of
Alfred Hitchcock's *Lifeboat* (1944)

Sammy [Davis Jr.] never complained about Sinatra's public
racist jokes about him. He smiled and took it. . . . He knew he
was a token. . . . Sammy realized he was lucky to be included
in Frank's Rat Pack, and he knew if he spoke up, his career
could be harmed by Frank, a powerful and vengeful man.

— ex-Rat Packer **PETER LAWFORD**
to *TV Radio Mirror* magazine

Richard Pryor was ready to put out a million-dollar
hit on [comedian/writer] Paul Mooney. He had
sufficient cause, . . . personal, don't ask me about it.
But then Pryor had that big, big drugs blow-up.

— comedian **GILBERT GOTTFRIED**

*

Hail the flaming freebase Richard Pryor Comet, flashing
through the Tinseltown night! Scar tissue, anyone?

— *Hollywood Babylon II* author **KENNETH
ANGER** on the drug-addled comedian

She was an accident waiting to happen. She had narcolepsy [falling asleep without warning], and a spell could happen to her any time. The fatal one happened behind the wheel.

— **CHRISTOPHER PENN** on acting teacher Peggy Feury, killed during a narcoleptic spell in a head-on car crash in 1985. He and his brother Sean were her students.

Dear World, I am leaving because I am bored. I feel I have lived long enough. I am leaving you with your worries in this sweet cesspool—good luck. Love, George

— suicide note of Oscar-winning actor **GEORGE SANDERS**, who died at 65 on the Spanish Riviera

My brother became an actor, . . . but above-average looks are required for an actress. My sister toyed with the idea. But when she said, "I've half a mind to become an actress," I told her, 'That's the other requirement.'

— **GEORGE SANDERS** (*All about Eve*)

People think actors are smarter than comedians. Let me tell you: lots of comedians write their own material. Actors don't. Otherwise they'd be playwrights or, um, movie-wrights.

— comedian **STANLEY MYRON HANDELMAN**

I'm not funny. What I am is brave.

— **LUCILLE BALL**

I'll have a double cheeseburger and a chocolate shake.

— comedian **PAUL LYNDE**, upon rolling his window down after a police chase on Sunset Boulevard that ended with the drunk driver's car jumping a curb onto the front lawn of a Beverly Hills mansion

If they're pretty, they choose acting. If not, comedy. So many comediennes are Sapphic. Even, or especially, if they have a man-chasing image. . . . Being a female comic must be the toughest showbiz job.

— **JIM BACKUS** (*Gilligan's Island*)

I was asked one time if Gilligan and the Skipper were lovers. That is the dumbest question I've ever been asked.

— **BOB "GILLIGAN" DENVER**

Puppets don't have a sexual orientation.

— **OFFICIAL PBS DENIAL** that Bert and Ernie are a gay couple. The very close fabric friends were based on a *Sesame Street* writer and his male partner. Besides, didn't Miss Piggy have a sexual orientation?

Being on American television talk shows is like walking a tightrope. The host wants me to be funny and, often, only not quite as funny as he is.

— Manhattan-based UK author **QUENTIN CRISP**

Americans are more forthright in their questions. A famous talk-show host asked me if I was wearing a wig? Rather than being tongue-tied at his rudeness, I somehow managed to politely say, "No, you see if this were a wig, it would look more natural."
— **QUENTIN CRISP**

✳

People warned me that for some younger male guests, to get on *Merv Griffin*, you had to get *on* Merv Griffin.
— ex–child star **GEORGE "FOGHORN" WINSLOW** (*Gentlemen Prefer Blondes*), who passed up the talk show

✳

I'll do a talk show if I want to make a point about something or I like the host. I won't do it to advertise my newest picture. . . . One thing that makes me hesitate is viewers tuning in not to hear what I have to say but only to see how I've aged or how much I weigh now.
— **MARLON BRANDO**

✳

I loved it that people were shocked when Marlon came on my show and kissed me on the lips. . . . And he's not a bad kisser.
— talk-show host **LARRY KING**

I was put on *Larry King Live* immediately after Liberace died. The show featured my new book *Conversations with My Elders*, which included a taped interview with Rock Hudson. The book didn't include Rock's confession that he and Liberace had had a brief affair in the early 1950s, when "Lee" was the bigger star. It was agreed that would not be made public till after both men's deaths. Anyway, at the time I had recently moved to Beverly Hills and was thinking of becoming an actor. So I asked King's producer to request that he not ask if I was gay. Back then, gay actors were unemployable. She said she would ask him and apparently did. The first thing King asks me is, "Are you gay?" I said no. I should not have said no. But then, Hollywood should not discriminate. It forced and it forces people to lie.

— author (hello) **BOZE HADLEIGH**

I knew a very talented, little-known stage actor that was recommended to producer Sam Spiegel for the lead in *Lawrence of Arabia*. I'm not sure if Spiegel interviewed him, but he rejected him because Spiegel was a homophobe, and the actor was a homosexual.

— author and critic **ROBIN WOOD**

I was interested in playing T. E. Lawrence, . . . an unusual personality and circumstances. The producer wanted me, then he didn't want me. . . . Decided that if he cast me, the audience and critics would think of it as *Brando of Arabia*.

— **MARLON BRANDO**

Child actors could be pushed around something awful, and boy actors had little future. Happily, my talents included writing; therefore my plays provided success as a playwright and adult actor.

— **NOËL COWARD** (also a songwriter, screenwriter, etc.)

✳

A lot of children, when their parents divorce, think they, not the adults, are at fault. You can imagine if a family's income derives largely from a TV child star, how that child feels when the series is canceled.

— psychotherapist **BETTY BERZON**

✳

What other business uses adopted children as publicity props? Whether it's a Joan Crawford with a set of four or a gay star and his wife with two. . . . It's ongoingly phony. Also sad. More so for the children.

— *Teen Bag* editor **LIL SMITH**

✳

If you think there's nothing to the numerous molestation charges against Michael Jackson—and all his pay-offs—watch the DVD documentary *Leaving Neverland*. It's not a puff piece, like those interviews with him and Lisa Marie Presley. It only presents facts.

— music executive **HOLLY LANE**

Michael Jackson was often photographed with Bubbles, his chimpanzee companion. After a space of time, you saw and heard nothing about Bubbles. . . . I found out he'd aged and gotten ugly, no longer photo-op cute, and was sold or given away—banished from Neverland, as it were.

— animal-rights activist **ALYSSA HUTTON**. Born in 1983, Bubbles was larger and less manageable by 2003, when he was transferred to an animal trainer, who shut down his business in 2004. Since 2005, Bubbles dwells in a Florida ape sanctuary.

We're very proud of Shemp.

— **MOE HOWARD** of the Three Stooges, regarding brother and fellow Stooge Shemp Howard being voted the ugliest man in Hollywood

When it was revealed that the male Corporal Klinger character on M*A*S*H wore a model 36B Miss High Rise bra, sales surged forward.

— underwear designer **PAT KURTZ**

Liz [Smith] has confided in friends that she finds Lisa Marie Presley hard as nails and utterly lacking in charm. Liz doesn't diss her in print because she wants to keep the channel open for stories on the none-too-happy Presley clan.

— Hollywood columnist **GEORGE CHRISTY**

I'm still a little disconcerted when I'm asked to sign a lady's bosom. . . . It's a challenge to write one's name on a quivering breast without using the other hand to steady it.
— TV Batman **ADAM WEST** in his memoirs

You can't have a star like that doin' stuff like that, spendin' their time. . . . If his fans were dumb enough to believe Elvis sat there and autographed each and every photograph, then I don't have sympathy for anyone so gullible.
— Colonel **TOM PARKER**

You're displaying some pretty bad judgment.
— Elvis Presley's personal physician, **GEORGE NICHOPOULOS** ("Dr. Nick"), prescriber of the 25-odd pills Elvis ingested daily. After the doc took away his pills, Presley reacted by shooting at him.

I'm not ashamed of it, and I'm not proud of it. It was perfectly legal until well into the '60s.
— **CARY GRANT** on having taken LSD more than once (but not admitting he took it to try to become heterosexual)

When I worked with [Cary Grant], I was surprised to learn he didn't like kissing scenes. To most leading men that's the frosting on the cake.
— **MARILYN MONROE**

Some men kiss and don't tell. Some kiss and tell. Cary Grant told but didn't kiss.

— Woolworth heiress **BARBARA HUTTON** on her ex-husband, to her son Lance

✳

I'm very loyal in relationships. Even when I go out with my mom, I don't look at other moms.

— comedian **GARRY SHANDLING**

✳

My mother said to me, "You're revolting. And on top of that you're not even very feminine." Well, that led me to the stage, which is an accepting and comfortable place. So in a way I have my mother to thank.

— **CAROL CHANNING**

✳

My mother was the real Wicked Witch of the West.

— **JUDY GARLAND**

✳

I found my way to the [Chateau Marmont hotel] elevator. I knocked on the door Mom told me to go to, and next thing I knew, Kirk Douglas was ushering me into his suite.

— **NATALIE WOOD**, recalling her encounter at 16 with the 38-year-old star: "He hurt me." About her mother's reaction to the violation: "Mom was sure it would have meant the end of my career if I'd caused trouble for Kirk Douglas. So of course [she said to] suck it up."

When I was very young, without my consent, my ears were pinned back [via plastic surgery] so I wouldn't share that famous physical trait with my real father.
— **JUDY LEWIS**, love child of married (to other people) costars Clark Gable and Loretta Young, who pretended Judy was adopted. Lewis eventually *told*, in her memoirs.

✳

It seems as if, if you don't want a book written about you, don't have a child! . . . I would have made a terrible parent. The first time my child didn't do what I wanted, I'd kill him.
— **KATHARINE HEPBURN**

✳

Apparently Stephen Sondheim stayed in the closet until his mother died.
— Broadway documentarian **RICK MCKAY**

✳

[Choreographer/director] Jerome Robbins gave in to columnist Ed Sullivan and his fellow witch hunters because he didn't want them to tell his mother he was gay.
— **RICK MCKAY**

✳

I got immense flak for saying [director] Blake Edwards was gay. . . . I was only stating what I thought the interviewer already knew. After that, my job was in jeopardy.
— **MAX BERCUTT**, head of Warner Bros. publicity for 15 years

I was desperate to be outed, but nobody would publicize
the fact. Lots of journalists still believe they're
protecting you by not putting it into their articles.
— actor-turned-playwright **KEITH CURRAN**

✳

Batgirl wasn't introduced during *Batman*'s third season merely to
add variety. There was pressure from ABC censors to add a third
wheel, a female one, to that inseparable male dynamic duo.
— cable-TV host and producer **CARL DAVID**

✳

You play a murderer, people don't suspect you might
be one. Play an alcoholic, there's possible suspicion.
. . . You play gay, most people wonder.
— **CHRISTOPHER REEVE**, who played gay in *Deathtrap*

✳

Actors, even minor ones, used to refuse to play gay. That is,
once it became legal even to depict gay characters. Then they
started winning awards for it . . . and could always declare
what a stretch it was and how proud of them their wives
were. Hollywood is Hollywood—money, ego, baloney.
— ICM agent **ED LIMATO**

✳

Partly to reassure general audiences, Tinseltown's habit is casting
heterosexuals in homosexual roles. Say, Robin Williams in *The
Birdcage*. . . . One right-wing closeted TV star took advantage of
the habit to play a supporting gay role in a movie. Most people and
some reviewers thought it proved he wasn't gay. He's gay. Maybe
not practicing any more, but he still wants what he's wanted.
— gay actor **TAYLOR NEGRON**

I was accosted in the streets and even slapped by angry ladies.
. . . The gentlemen usually hissed or spat. Some of them leered.
— silent-movie vamp **THEDA BARA**, whose screen
specialty was luring and ruining married men

✳

If a straight actor, a star, has to do a gay love scene—'cause
nonstars don't do love scenes—it can be one of two things:
He's nervous he can't do it and will embarrass himself,
or he's afraid he might do it too avidly and enjoy it.
— director **JOEL SCHUMACHER**

✳

Cecil B. DeMille had a foot fetish. I drove him mad with
my feet and actually used my bare feet to get better roles.
— PAULETTE GODDARD

✳

My husband took me to see the X-rated, all-nude
play *Oh, Calcutta!* At intermission he turned to me
and asked, "How come there are no erections?"
"Dummy," I told him, "these are professionals."
— JOAN RIVERS

✳

Elvis disliked confrontations, . . . never wanted to be the
bad guy. . . . He preferred someone else to fire somebody for
him. When he got mad enough to kill the karate instructor
he felt betrayed him, he wanted one of us to go shoot
the guy dead for him. . . . Elvis was touchy about what
people thought of him, not just the big wide public.
— bodyguard **RED WEST**, eventual coauthor
of a book about Presley and his court

When [my managers] the Rosses stole me from my
mother and started making me into a child star, I did
think about suicide. Kids do. . . . One thing I learned is
you cannot commit suicide by holding your breath!
— **PATTY DUKE**, who won an Oscar in her early teens

✳

Olivia Newton-John and I were together for years. After
singing, she hit it big in *Grease*, . . . then I produced
her solo movie, *Xanadu* [1980]. The record was a big
hit, but the movie for sure wasn't, so I was fired.
Stars blame the manager or agent. . . . They should blame
audiences that don't show up. And maybe the material.
Xanadu was kind of shlocky, but *Grease* was shlockier.
— manager **LEE KRAMER**

✳

The question is sometimes asked, Why are so many actors gay?
. . . We start learning to act as children. We have to *pass*, . . .
pretend to be what we're not, to live more smoothly—in some
cases less violently—with society, starting with our own families.
— **RON VAWTER** (*Silence of the Lambs*)

✳

Acting is an emotional, you could even say feminine
business. Maybe this accounts for there being fewer lesbian
actresses than gay actors. But a lot of leading men do feel
ashamed or embarrassed about acting, even putting the
profession down. But they stay on for the money, honey.
— acting coach **TARA MESSER**

Acting really isn't a fit business for a man to be in.
— **SPENCER TRACY**

Scratch an actor, and you'll find an actress.
— **DOROTHY PARKER**

My initial interest was poetry. . . . I imagined I would become a writer or historian. . . . I don't state it with pride: "I am an actor."
— **RICHARD BURTON**

I remember an eye-opening Richard Burton interview in *People* or someplace. He said most actors are sexually insecure or secretly gay. They "cover it with drink," he said.
— talk-show host **VIRGINIA GRAHAM**, who eventually revealed her late husband was gay

It came as a surprise to young Burt when an older, drunken Spencer Tracy came on to him. . . . Several long-ago Hollywood stars repressed themselves while sober and were gay only while drunk. That deep self-repression was why several of them drank.
— Reynolds friend and director **HAL NEEDHAM**

I was from Montana, so Hollywood was where I finally started meeting and liking all sorts of people. Blacks, Jews, gay men, . . . lesbians I'd already met. It was exhilarating and educational.
— **PATRICIA NELL WARREN**, lesbian author of the best-selling gay-male novel *The Front Runner*, which Paul Newman tried in vain to film

Actors come from everywhere. We mix with others. We
evolve. We work with and are indebted to a large percentage
of gays and Jews. What are we supposed to do? Regress
and become narrow again—intolerant and bigoted?
— **DAVID DUKES**, responding to Republican
politicians' charges that actors are "too liberal"

I'm not black, and I'm not white, and I'm not
pink, and I'm not green. Eartha Kitt has no color,
and that is how barriers are broken.
— biracial singer/actress **EARTHA KITT**

Black couples on the screen or in print advertising typically show
a lighter actress than the actor. . . . She's closer to white. This is
standard casting, whether she represents "wife" or "girlfriend."
It discriminates against darker African American actresses and
is very sexist. For him, the skin shade doesn't matter at all.
— talent manager **FRED LEMACK**

One of our several hundred *Match Game* contestants was a young
lady named Kirstie Alley. . . . I wouldn't really call her a lady.
She was strikingly attractive but unwarrantedly arrogant and
foul-mouthed. Twice she farted on-set but didn't apologize.
She didn't communicate a desire to be an actress, but she already
had the necessary hide of a rhinoceros and manners of a hyena.
— game-show director **IRA SKUTCH**

With showbiz parents and the Liz Taylor scandal, I
grew up quickly. By my teens, I was 30-something. . . .
I inherited negative attitudes like entitlement. When I
learned I wasn't their first choice [to play Princess Leia in
Star Wars], I was initially disappointed and peeved.

— **CARRIE FISHER**, daughter of Debbie Reynolds and
Eddie Fisher, who left Debbie to marry Elizabeth Taylor.
Princess Leia was earlier offered to Jodie Foster.

Whitney Houston was tough and ambitious. She would
never have come out. . . . There was an '80s movie starring
two actresses. Houston was having an affair with one of
them. She may not have been aware the costars were already
having an affair. When one found out, she punched out her
costar. . . . The movie had to shut down for over a week.
Much later, both actresses came out. Black lesbians
and bisexual girls needed a role model, . . . but
Whitney was me, me, me. Closeted unto death.

— stuntwoman **PAULA DELL**

It took me several years to realize I didn't have
much talent for acting, . . . but by then I couldn't
give it up because I had become too famous.

— Argentine actor and Hollywood star **FERNANDO LAMAS**

Others said I made the wrong decision, but it was right for me. . . . I've learned to ride out the bad and enjoy the good. In place of bitterness, I'm happy for Gloria [Stuart]. We both did a number of classic 1930s horror pictures, and she deserved a big comeback. Now her name is almost as well-known as mine.

— **FAY WRAY**, who declined to costar in *Titanic*

Karen [Carpenter] never learned to love herself, partly because her mother didn't love her. Some mothers won't cheer their daughters on.

— **PAUL BUCKMASTER**, music orchestrator

If you're somebody who's happy in your work, avoid acting. Most of the time, actors aren't acting; they're seeking or hoping for work. Even stars like Henry Fonda would say they feared that their latest role would be their last.

— Chicago casting director **JANE ALDERMAN**

An actor can be happiest if he likes his wife and loves his director.

— **VIC MORROW**, who last acted in the ill-fated *Twilight Zone: The Movie*

If you are unhappy before fame, you will probably be unhappy during fame.

— Buddhist Oscar-winner Dr. **HAING S. NGOR**

Just try to be happy. Unhappiness starts with wanting to be *happier*.

— author **SAM LEVENSON**, who added, "If you die in an elevator, be sure to push the Up button."

9

- - - - - - - - -

Politics

In politics, a friend is a person with the same enemies you have.
— Southern politician **GEORGE WALLACE**

✳

If you want a friend in Washington, get a dog.
— President **HARRY S. TRUMAN**

✳

The man with the best job in the country is the
vice president. All he has to do is get up every
morning and say, "How's the president?"
— comedian **WILL ROGERS**, who died in a 1935 plane crash

✳

[It's] not worth a bucket of warm piss.
— Vice President **JOHN NANCE GARNER** (1933–1941) on the
vice-presidency. For decades the euphemism *warm spit* was used.

✳

I am in control here. As of now, I am in
control here in the White House.
— Secretary of State and General **ALEXANDER
HAIG** after President Reagan was shot, unaware
he was only fourth in the line of succession

✳

Politics is perhaps the only profession for which
no preparation is thought necessary.
— **ROBERT LOUIS STEVENSON**

✳

In politics, stupidity is not a handicap.
— **NAPOLEON BONAPARTE**

Trees cause more pollution than automobiles do.
— **RONALD REAGAN** in 1981

✳

It needs to be said that the poor are poor
because they don't have enough money.
— Sir **KEITH JOSEPH**, British Minister of
Health, enlightening the nation in 1970

✳

I think Britain could benefit from a fascist leader. . . .
I believe very strongly in fascism. People have always
responded with greater efficiency under a regimental
leader. . . . Adolf Hitler was one of the first rock stars.
— **DAVID BOWIE** in 1975

✳

If David Bowie's latest persona is the Thin White Duke, he's going
to give a bad name to whites, thin people, and peers of the realm.
— fellow singer **FREDDIE MERCURY**

✳

If I had been an Italian, I am sure I would have been with
you from the beginning to the end. . . . Your movement
[fascism] has abroad rendered a service to the whole world.
— **WINSTON CHURCHILL** in a letter to
dictator Mussolini, pre–World War II

✳

The illegal we do immediately. The
unconstitutional takes a little longer.
— **HENRY KISSINGER**

They devalued the Nobel Peace Prize by giving it to Henry Kissinger. Beyond belief, beneath contempt. . . . The man is a war criminal. Read up, if you don't believe it.

— **GEORGE CARLIN**

✳

Democracy: Use it, people, or lose it!

— Congresswoman **BELLA ABZUG**

✳

Not a true democracy. Their Electoral College has, to date [2021], disallowed the people's votes five times. Five times out of five, it awarded the presidency to the Conservative—in their case, Republican—candidate.

— UK political analyst **DAVID WILSON**

✳

That "college" goes far back to when blacks were slaves and women couldn't vote. How can it yet and still be considered more relevant than the votes of American citizens?

— journalist **SCOTT TIMBERG**

✳

That George Washington was not a scholar is certain. That he is too illiterate, unlearned, unread for his station is equally beyond dispute.

— **JOHN ADAMS**, the second US president.

✳

He is distrustful, obstinate, excessively vain, and takes no counsel from anyone.

— third US president **THOMAS JEFFERSON** on John Adams

They say I was a terrible president [1948–1952] of Cuba. That may be true. But I was the best president Cuba ever had.

— **CARLOS PRIO**, who in 1977, while exiled in Miami, fatally shot himself. Cuba's leaders have been uniformly dismal.

✳

It's generally thought JFK and the USA won the Cuban missile crisis, making Russia withdraw its missiles from Cuba. What's less known in the US is that Russia then forced removal of American Jupiter missiles from Turkey that were within striking distance of Moscow. Naturally, both sides claimed victory in the matter.

— UK historical novelist **PATRICK O'BRIAN**

✳

The truths about JFK's philandering were bound to reach the public. Likewise, Johnson. What's surprising is that for such a homely man, LBJ seemed to be at it as often as Kennedy.

— journalist **SHANA ALEXANDER**

✳

Frankly I don't mind not being president. I just mind that somebody else is.

— Senator **EDWARD M. KENNEDY**

✳

Another spoiled Kennedy brat. No loss. . . .
He died living it up in Florida.

— far-right "father of combat TV" **WALLY GEORGE** on David Kennedy, son of senator and presidential candidate Robert F. Kennedy, who died at 28 in 1984 of a drug overdose

David was a boy when his father was assassinated in
1968. Recurring nightmares led to experimenting with
drugs. . . . Injuries from a 1973 car accident led to
addictive painkillers. . . . He traveled to Florida to see his
grandmother Rose Kennedy, who'd suffered a stroke.
. . . The autopsy found three drugs in David's system:
cocaine, a painkiller, and a tranquilizer.
— columnist **SHIRLEY EDER**

✳

William McKinley has no more backbone than a chocolate éclair.
— President **THEODORE ROOSEVELT** in 1901
on the future third-assassinated US president

✳

I have noticed that nothing that I never
said ever did me any harm.
— President **CALVIN COOLIDGE**

✳

How can they tell?
— **DOROTHY PARKER** in 1933, upon being
informed that Calvin Coolidge had died

✳

I think the only hope this country has is Nixon's assassination.
— **GROUCHO MARX** in 1971 in *Flash* magazine.
The FBI reopened its anti-Groucho file, bulging
with notes from the blacklist years, and branded
the octogenarian a "national security risk."

Why change Dicks in the middle of a screw. Reelect Nixon in '72.
— POPULAR BATHROOM GRAFFITO

✳

You know, the difficulty with a president when he makes a statement is that everybody checks to see whether it is true.
— RICHARD NIXON

✳

Richard Nixon is the kind of politician who would cut down a redwood tree, then mount its stump for a speech on conservation.
— 1950s presidential candidate **ADLAI STEVENSON**

✳

If the Republicans stop telling lies about the Democrats, we will stop telling the truth about them.
— ADLAI STEVENSON

✳

I'm strictly for Stevenson. I don't dig the intellectual bit, but I'm telling you, man, he knows the most.
— **ELVIS PRESLEY**. The considerably more intelligent candidate lost twice, in 1952 and 1956, to Dwight D. Eisenhower.

✳

The fellow doesn't know any more about politics than a pig knows about Sunday.
— **HARRY TRUMAN** on his successor, Eisenhower, an army general

✳

Politics is too serious a matter to be left to the politicians.
— general and French president **CHARLES DE GAULLE**

Dewey Defeats Truman

— erroneous November 3, 1948, **FRONT-PAGE BANNER HEADLINE** of the *Chicago Daily Tribune*, whose presidential-election coverage relied overly on polls

✳

He's a hero but avoids and fears publicity.

— **HARVEY MILK** on friend and ex-Marine Oliver Sipple, who blocked an assassination attempt against President Gerald Ford in San Francisco in 1975. When his midwestern family learned Sipple was gay, they cut him off, and their church shunned them. Sipple sued several newspapers for $15 million, but after nine years, California's Supreme Court dismissed the case, stating that he became a public figure the day he saved the president's life.

✳

Why did that gay guy go out of his way to save Ford? What did Ford or Nixon or any Republican ever do for gay people, except try and get us fired and use us as scapegoats? And what did that guy get out of it?

— record producer **BOB CAVIANO**

✳

Why on Earth would anyone support a party that doesn't want them to have any rights? That in fact does not want them to exist?

— gay businessman **DAVE FOREST**, regarding gay Republicans

✳

Two presidents entered the White House as bachelors. One left it a married man—Grover Cleveland, 49, wed a 21-year-old there. James Buchanan, our 15th president, was a "lifelong bachelor," almost certainly gay. His niece performed hospitality or "First Lady" duties.

— history teacher **STEVE HUNIU**

They were gay but we don't know if they were lovers or boyfriends.
. . . President James Buchanan's other half was Senator William Rufus
King . . . sometimes called, behind his back, the president's wife.

— UCSB professor **FELIPE POWELL**

✳

I'll tell you what the coloreds want. It's three things: first, a tight
pussy; second, loose shoes; and third, a warm place to shit.

— **EARL BUTZ**, Nixon's and Ford's secretary of
agriculture, in 1976. Postcomment, Butz resigned.

✳

I've been called worse things by better men.

— Canadian prime minister **PIERRE TRUDEAU**
after Nixon called him an "asshole"

✳

Richard Nixon impeached himself.
He gave us Gerald Ford as his revenge.

— Congresswoman **BELLA ABZUG**

✳

I have often been accused of putting my foot in my
mouth, but I will never put my hand in your pockets.

— Nixon's vice president **SPIRO AGNEW** in 1969. He
later resigned after accepting political kickbacks.

✳

Politicians should wear sponsor jackets like NASCAR
drivers. Then we know who owns them.

— **ROBIN WILLIAMS**

✳

One cannot accomplish anything without fanaticism.

— ex-actress **EVA PERÓN**, "spiritual leader"
and would-be vice-president of Argentina

In 1946, [Tyrone Power] and I went on a Latin American
goodwill tour. We met Juan Perón, Argentina's president,
and Evita. Perón said very little, but after a long
chat, it became clear to us that if Evita were offered a
Hollywood contract, she'd have left her husband.

— actor **CESAR ROMERO**

Nobody not [in the military] did more to oppose
the Nazis than we in Hollywood.

— **WALT DISNEY**, the only studio head who
welcomed "Hitler's golden girl," director Leni
Riefenstahl, when she visited Hollywood in 1938

Attila the Hen.

— writer and Member of Parliament **CLEMENT FREUD**,
grandson of Sigmund, on Prime Minister Margaret Thatcher

The response to male chauvinism about female heads of state
is, simply, can women do any worse than men have done?

— novelist **JACKIE COLLINS**

Extremist males are threatened by women who speak
up. . . . They hate male liberals but want to destroy
female liberals by any slanderous or libelous means.

— Australian journalist **LILLIAN ROXON**

When the debate is lost, slander becomes the tool of the losers.

— **SOCRATES**

From Colonel and Mrs. George S. Patton III—Peace on Earth
— 1968 **CHRISTMAS CARD GREETING**, beneath a
photo of Viet Cong corpses, dismembered and in a pile

✳

Victory for the Viet Cong would mean ultimately the
destruction of freedom of speech for all men for all time,
not only in Asia but in the United States, as well.
— alarmist attorney and former vice president
RICHARD NIXON in 1965

✳

If we quit Vietnam, tomorrow we'll be fighting in Hawaii,
and next week we'll have to fight in San Francisco.
— alarmist president **LYNDON JOHNSON** in 1967

✳

I have taken all the manure that has been
thrown on me and used it as fertilizer.
— biracial singer/actress **EARTHA KITT**, who was
boycotted in the United States after she expressed
opposition to the war in Vietnam at a ladies' luncheon
hosted by First Lady Lady Bird Johnson

✳

I, too, was against the war in Vietnam. Do you know
what they called it in East Asia? The War of American
Aggression. . . . Opposing a government is not opposing
your country. If a 1930s German was anti-Hitler, did
that make him or her anti-German? Get real!
— PETER FONDA

We're still calling them "Indians" because in 1492
Columbus thought he'd landed in India. It's time
to correct that error. . . . *Native Americans* isn't
necessarily politically correct; it's just correct.
— MARLON BRANDO

All the problems we face in the US today can be
traced to an unenlightened immigration policy
on the part of the American Indian.
— comedian **PAT PAULSEN**

We are not interested in the possibilities
of defeat. They do not exist.
— QUEEN VICTORIA in 1900, about the Boer
War in South Africa, which Britain later lost

I am not worried about the deficit. It is
big enough to take care of itself.
— RONALD REAGAN

It's official now. Nancy Reagan is going to be
the world's first artificial heart donor.
— comedian **GEORGE KIRBY**

Her image is grandmotherly white-haired nice. I've
met Barbara Bush. It's image, not reality.
— cultural critic **GERSHON LEGMAN**

If women were in the Constitution, a special amendment
to grant them the vote would have been unnecessary.
The Equal Rights Amendment is still needed.

— **VALERIE HARPER**

"Liberty and justice for all," . . . yet something as fair and
simple as the Equal Rights Amendment was defeated.
The Right totally misrepresented it, like scaring people
about no more men's rooms or ladies' rooms.
The media, playing neutral, went right along. The media loves
controversy. . . . This should *not* have been controversial.

— author **ALEX COMFORT**

I applaud President Nixon's comprehensive statement
which clearly demonstrates again that the president
was not involved with the Watergate matter.

— **GEORGE BUSH** in 1974, months before
Richard Nixon was forced to resign

Nixon sought revenge on Newport, Rhode Island, and
on John Lennon. . . . His southern crony [Senator] Strom
Thurmond tried to help him deport Lennon because
of his antiwar activism. It took years in court, but we
uncovered their illegal secret schemes, . . . and we won.
Unfortunately, Nixon impacted the economy of Rhode Island,
a state that didn't embrace him in the presidential election.

— John Lennon's attorney **LEON WILDES** in 2004

Gandhi has been assassinated. In my humble
opinion, a bloody good thing but far too late.

— imperialist **NOËL COWARD** in his diary, on the saintly
Mahatma ("Great Soul") Gandhi, whose nonviolent
efforts helped India gain independence from Britain

✳

The most chilling thing I ever read, around 2000, was from
some Chinese general. . . . I paraphrase: We can afford to
lose 300 million people. You cannot. You would be left
with very few people. We'd still have about a billion.

— author **WILLIAM PETER BLATTY**
(*The Exorcist*) in the *New Times* (Los Angeles)

✳

I hate very few things or people. . . . One is the governments
of Turkey, a supposedly modern Islamic democracy. It
slaughtered over a million and a half Armenian Christians
yet still denies the fact. . . . By contrast, Germany long
ago acknowledged and apologized for the Holocaust.

— TV personality **ARLENE FRANCIS**
(née Kazanjian), whose paternal grandparents were
killed in Turkey, to *Asbarez* newspaper in Los Angeles

✳

The real horror, after America had fought European
fascists like Hitler and Mussolini in World War II, was
that the domestic ones could now put a stop to you.

— stage star **HERSCHEL BERNARDI**
(*Fiddler on the Roof*) on political blacklisting

Communism was the pretext for the witch hunters. When did you ever see a communist movie? Those US fascists' real goal, then as now, and using Hollywood for publicity, was to get rid of as many liberals, Jews, gays, and other minorities as they could.

— blacklisted movie composer **ELMER BERNSTEIN**

The only -ism Hollywood believes in is plagiarism.

— playwright **LILLIAN HELLMAN**

Martin Luther pioneered Protestantism and opposed the [Catholic] Church's corruption . . . but was himself morally bankrupt. . . . While he acknowledged that Jesus and the apostles were Jewish, in 1543 he published a lengthy screed, *On the Jews and Their Lies*, that rivals anything Hitler wrote.

— playwright and screenwriter **LEONARD GERSHE**

Is he a Catholic or a Christian?

— **GLADYS PRESLEY**, after hearing about son Elvis's intended manager Tom Parker. Most of the world's Christians are Catholics.

Some Americans confuse Martin Luther with Martin Luther King Jr. Martin Luther later influenced the Nazis. . . . He preached every sort of cruelty, including burning down Jewish homes with Jews still in them. That this is unknown or ignored is shameful.

— journalist **SHANA ALEXANDER**

We will drive them into the sea!
— Egyptian dictator **GAMAL ABDUL NASSER**, speaking of Israel in 1968

A free society is a society where it is safe to be unpopular.
— American ambassador to the United Nations **ADLAI STEVENSON II**

I have a half-Egyptian friend who can't return there because he is also half-Jewish and openly gay. He could easily be killed there for either reason, . . . and authorities would look the other way.
— stand-up comic **CARMINE WESTGATE**

In 2019, the Muslim sultan of [oil-rich] Brunei created a law to have LGBTQ people stoned. It didn't stir up anything near the reaction against apartheid in South Africa, and apartheid wasn't about killing people. Any country's minorities will always experience *some* discrimination. . . . Blacks here have the advantage: they can move to Africa and become part of the majority. I'm gay. I don't have that advantage anywhere.
— publicist **HOWARD BRAGMAN**

Slavery has existed in every civilization, and most slaves were prisoners of war, the same race as their captors. . . . Yes, the British and Americans shipped slaves in from Africa, but they were sold into slavery there by their fellow blacks. . . . Look into the historical record.

— playwright **REGINALD ROSE**
(*Twelve Angry Men*) to reporter Harold Fairbanks

✳

I am free of all prejudices. I hate everyone equally.

— **W. C. FIELDS**

✳

One test of democracy is whether the gays and the lesbians are included when it comes to human rights. . . . Most of the countries that still punish them are Islamic or black, the punishment ranging from prison to death.

— Nigerian teacher **PETER OLADAPO**

✳

Israel has built itself up into a developed country and a democracy. But dictatorships in the region still use the excuse of anti-Israel hate—three-quarters of a century later—to distract from their own impoverished economies, overpopulation, and lack of human rights at home.

— US-based Iranian banker **ARDESHIR MAHSID**

I have a Catholic friend who felt bad when she
was excommunicated. I told her she'd been evicted
from a club she wanted to leave anyway. I mean,
in Islam if you switch, the penalty is death.
— *Hill Street Blues* producer **STEVEN BOCHCO**
in 2017 to columnist George Christy

✳

There is [*sic*] not enough troops in the army to force the southern
people to break down segregation and admit the Negro race into
our theaters, into our swimming pools, and into our churches.
— Senator **STROM THURMOND** in 1948;
he remained in office until 2003.

✳

These are not bad people. All they are concerned about
is to see that their sweet little girls are not required to sit
in school alongside some big overgrown Negroes.
— President **DWIGHT D. EISENHOWER** at a White
House dinner in 1954, defending segregation proponents

✳

Eisenhower warned against the growing military-industrial
complex, but he also invaded Guatemala on the advice of
a golfing friend who was an American banana baron and in
1953 issued executive order 10450, which made thousands
of lesbians and gays ineligible for government jobs and led to
mass firings. . . . That order was only dismantled in stages, the
last two under the Clinton and Obama administrations.
— military essayist **BOYD MCDONALD**

Now listen, you queer. Stop calling me a crypto-Nazi, or I'll sock you in your goddamn face, and you'll stay plastered.

— **WILLIAM F. BUCKLEY** to Gore Vidal during a live telecast from the 1968 Democratic Convention in Chicago. Columnist Herb Caen remarked, "Buckley is jealous of Vidal. . . . Buckley has never written a book that anyone can name."

Closeting occasionally yields a positive result. . . . The state's voters didn't realize earlier they were electing a gay governor. There was minimal awareness of gay men then. Later, when he ran and won, it had to be as a married man. . . . He was a good governor, and he's a pretty good guy. The marriage is political. It served its purpose.

— Hollywood publicist **ANDREA JAFFE**

There are two kinds of rich. [President] Franklin Roosevelt was called a "traitor to his class" because he worked for the average man rather than the rich. . . . And then there are the rich—born rich or became rich—who work for the rich and don't give a shit about the average person or the poor.

— journalist **ROBERT TIMBERG**

When he does smile, he looks as if he's just evicted a widow.

— columnist **MIKE ROYKO** on Senator Bob Dole

He has never met a tax he hasn't hiked.

— fellow Republican **JACK KEMP** on Bob Dole

Black, white, Jew, gentile, we're all working for one cause:
to figure out how you became governor [of California].
— comedian **DON RICKLES** at a Ronald Reagan roast in 1974

✳

Ronald Reagan must love poor people, because
he's creating so many more of them.
— Senator **EDWARD KENNEDY**

✳

It's stupid, it's cruel, it's elitism. . . . "Trickle-
down economics," my foot!
— economist **ANGIE DONATO**

✳

A working man voting for Ronald Reagan is like
a chicken voting for Colonel Sanders.
— Senator **PAUL SARBANES**

✳

A very substantial segment of Americans have the propensity
of voting their prejudices rather than their own interests.
— UK editor and political commentator
ANTHONY HOWARD

✳

You have to have been a Republican to know
how good it is to be a Democrat.
— **JACQUELINE KENNEDY ONASSIS**,
who hailed from a rich family

I'm a liberal. . . . Don't call me left wing. Not if that
implies communism, which is anti-liberty.
— movie star **EDWARD G. ROBINSON** to columnist
Dorothy Manners. *Left wing* and *right wing* harks back
to the French Revolution's National Assembly, where
representatives of the average people sat to the president's
left and those of the royalists sat to his right.

✳

There they are. See no evil, hear no evil, and . . . evil.
— **BOB DOLE**, watching ex-presidents Carter, Ford, and
Nixon standing side by side at a White House event

✳

Patriotism is when love of your own people comes first;
nationalism, when hate for people other than your own comes first.
— **CHARLES DE GAULLE**

✳

We learn from history that we do not learn from history.
— philosopher **GEORG HEGEL**

✳

Politics have no relation to morals.
— **NICCOLO MACHIAVELLI** in *The Prince* (1532)

✳

You can state with conviction that Canada is better
than the USA, Russia, and all the rest. Name one other
country that's gotten rid of its nuclear weapons.
— Canadian actor **JOHN CANDY**

10

Pants on Fire!

I am not a crook.

— RICHARD NIXON

✳

I never wore makeup.

— ex-actor **RONALD REAGAN**

✳

I experienced combat in Vietnam.

— actor **BRIAN DENNEHY**, who didn't participate in the war in Vietnam

✳

I rarely discuss my experiences and never boast of them. . . . Courage and bravery were merely the order of the day.

— UK actor **TREVOR HOWARD**, whose impressive World War II record was revealed as a sham after he died

✳

It's understandable.

— author **ART AVEILHE**, defending the lie of an actress who claimed an affair with Rock Hudson to help sell her memoirs, published shortly after Hudson's death

✳

Living in Hollywood, I do have gay friends, but no, . . . I'm not. . . . No.

— **ROCK HUDSON**, a few years before disclosure of his AIDS condition

✳

We were engaged.

— **LIBERACE**, after the death of ice-skater-turned-movie-star Sonja Henie

I had to sue. . . . Their lies could have stopped my career cold.

— **LIBERACE**, who thrice sued periodicals for truthfully
noting his homosexuality and three times won. It's no
longer defamatory to write that someone is not straight.

My divorces have been painful things
which I prefer not to speak about.

— secretly gay **RAYMOND BURR** (*Perry Mason*), who
had one divorce and one male partner for more than 30
years but fabricated extra divorces and a "son who died"

There was no impropriety whatsoever in my
acquaintanceship with Miss [Christine] Keeler.

— **JOHN PROFUMO**, British minister of defense, lying in
the House of Commons in 1963. The ensuing sex scandal
toppled the government of Prime Minister Harold Macmillan.

Even a president should make time for romance.

— **RICHARD NIXON**, whose confidant Bebe Rebozo
told more than one mutual friend that Nixon had admitted
to not sleeping with wife Pat for more than 15 years

We don't lie. We put our own interpretation on what the truth is.

— Reagan national security advisor **ROBERT
MCFARLANE**, quoted in *Propaganda Review*

Making up presidential quotes is not lying. When you're
a press secretary, you develop a bond of understanding
with the president so that you think like the president.
I knew those quotes were the way he felt.

— **LARRY SPEAKES**, press secretary to Ronald Reagan

✳

We need more honesty in politics.

— **RONALD REAGAN**, who at the 1992 Republican
National Convention attributed words to Abraham
Lincoln that Lincoln never said or wrote

✳

I have no political ambition for myself or for my children.

— **JOSEPH P. KENNEDY** in 1936

✳

By a landslide, the people of the United States
elected me to the presidency of this country.

— **JOHN F. KENNEDY** in 1963. He won by about 0.2
percent of the popular vote, the closest margin since
1916—not that the popular vote always counts.

✳

Don't pay any attention to any of the drivel you hear
about me and Jack Kennedy. It doesn't mean a thing.

— **JACKIE BOUVIER**, engaged to one John
Husted. A year later she married John F. Kennedy.

✳

Mr. Onassis is a good friend. . . . He is just a friend.

— **JACKIE KENNEDY**, weeks before wedding Aristotle Onassis

Barbara [Walters] and I have an understanding. . . . Marriage
is not everything. I don't know if she's in love with me,
[but] I do feel she's the most special woman in my life.
— attorney and anti-gay gay man **ROY COHN**, who "dated"
Walters for a cover. Cohn, who was also an anti-Semitic Jew, was
a prominent aide to political witch-hunter Joseph McCarthy.
Eventually disbarred, he died—despite loud denials—of AIDS.

The air-conditioning remained on throughout the interview,
causing an unusual noise in the background. . . . It couldn't
be turned off because the lights on [Michael] Jackson were
so hot that his thick pancake makeup and lipstick would
have melted and his false eyelashes would have come off.
— **ANONYMOUS ABC-TV SOUNDMAN** present at the
taping of Jackson's and Lisa Marie Presley's joint interview

Michael Jackson threw a temper tantrum when Lisa Marie's
two-year-old son pulled off his wig. Although she admonished
him, Michael stormed out and took a jet to Paris with
two young boys whom he had taken on trips before.
The boys stayed in the hotel room with Jackson
and accompanied him to Euro Disneyland.
— *SPY* MAGAZINE in 1996

For the majority of people, the use of
tobacco has a beneficial effect.
— Los Angeles surgeon **IAN MACDONALD**
in 1963, quoted in *Newsweek*

Sugar is not addictive and is good for all ages.
— Belgian chocolate designer **ALAIN TROUP**. Sugar activates D2 dopamine receptors and creates a short-term high that precedes a slump and the wish to repeat the high.

✳

We [ignore] commercials, but don't be overimpressed by claims from major outfits. The UN's World Health Organization declared coffee "possibly carcinogenic" for about 25 years, despite huge and mounting evidence to the contrary. . . . The WHO didn't remove coffee from its "Possibly Cancer Causing" list until 2016.
— university nutritionist **BERNADETTE MAZZO**

✳

The Nixon flunkies' grotesque lie insults public intelligence.
— nutritionist/author **ADELLE DAVIS** on that administration declaring Wheaties to be less nutritious than cereals like Clackers, Kaboom, and Froot Loops

✳

Louis Pasteur's theory of germs is ridiculous and fiction.
— **PIERRE PACHET**, French physiology professor, in 1872

✳

Mr. Darwin's theory of evolution will never be proven.
— **CHURCH OF ENGLAND PAMPHLET**, ca. 1870

✳

Atheists don't believe in gods or the traditional male sky god. We seek answers to human existence and the mysteries of the universe. But unlike the others, we don't make up answers.
— director **ROBERT ALTMAN**

Believe those myths you wish. Just don't try and convince me of them. And above all, don't pretend that they're "education."
— **STEVE ALLEN**, original *Tonight Show* host

Religions abound with fiction. If the fiction does no evil, let it stand. But if the fiction leads to the persecution and murder of those who don't share it, it should be opposed.
— Armenian (Christian) refugee from Iran
SHARONA AVANESSYAN

His type is precisely why outing had to finally happen and become a social-justice movement. . . . He was pastor of a church in the Northwest for some 30 years, loudly preaching lies and hatred against gay people. Off the pulpit, he was a closet case pursuing younger men and youths. He was finally exposed and booted out and died denying he was gay.
— publicist **HOWARD BRAGMAN**

And then there was the "reverend"—natch—who founded some homophobic activist group decades ago, then got caught returning from a vacation with a male prostitute. The rev's excuse was he hired the guy to carry his luggage 'cause he'd had surgery. Oh, what a tangled, self-hating web.
— former juvenile Disney star **TOMMY KIRK**

The worst are so-called ex-gays. Most sooner or later get caught, cruising on Grindr, sighted or photographed cruising in a gay bar, and so forth. Their lies do real harm because some people believe them, then try and "convert" their LGBT kids through damaging and often traumatizing quack "therapy."

— psychologist **CHARLES SILVERSTEIN**

President [Lyndon] Johnson uttered the biggest political lie of the second half of the 20th century, about "them" attacking "us" in the Gulf of Tonkin. That started, big time, the Vietnam War . . . and later involved the illegal and needless bombing of Vietnam's neighboring countries and untold human misery and death.

— historian **JEAN DUPONT**

I have no more territorial ambitions in Europe.

— **ADOLF HITLER** in 1938, after invading several countries and three months before invading Poland, thus starting World War II

Hitler said big lies were more convincing than little lies if repeated often enough. . . . German Jews served in Germany's military disproportionately during World War I. Yet Hitler ranted and raved that they betrayed Germany and were enemies, until it became an axe-grinding truth among his angry, frustrated followers.

— political columnist **MOLLY IVINS**

Create an enemy for ignorant people to hate, and you
can hold power and basically have a free hand.
— **BURT LANCASTER**, ACLU member

I keep seeing "Fear of a Black Planet" on T-shirts. . . . There are
more people in China than there are blacks, [including] African
Americans, but not north Africa, which is mostly not black.
— **DAVID WOLPER**, producer of *Roots*, to
Scarlet Street editor Richard Valley

Ethnic cleansing.
— **FREQUENTLY MISUSED PHRASE**, for example,
during the Serbian-Bosnian conflict, whose differences
weren't ethnic—the two groups weren't visually distinct—
but partly linguistic and primarily religious

＊

Fat Buddha Bar
— the sign on **A SAN FRANCISCO ESTABLISHMENT**.
The historical Buddha ("Enlightened One") was not fat.
Myriad seated, fat male statues represent a Chinese version
of Santa Claus whose belly is rubbed for good luck.

＊

Krakatoa, East of Java
— 1969 **MOVIE TITLE**. The island volcano is west of Java, and
its 1883 explosion was the loudest noise in recorded history.

Nine men are about to change history.
— **MOVIE TAGLINE** of *U-571*, the 2000 Hollywood
movie denounced in Parliament as an insult to the
Royal Navy. The flick substituted American characters
for the real-life World War II British heroes.

Of course Hollywood should include black actors but not
when it contradicts historical facts. . . . The [2006] movie *300*
is about events in Greece 2,500 years ago. Early on, a black
man appears and announces, "I am Persian." That is absurd.
That is just one example that perverts historical truth
and makes filmgoers even less knowledgeable.
— Iranian producer **REZA KHODADADI** on UK radio

The true villain was Henry VII, father of Henry VIII.
Shakespeare *had* to lie when he wrote up Richard III as a
villain. He wrote his play under the Tudor dynasty, founded
by Henry VII, who got rid of Richard, then spread lies
about him to legitimize his takeover. Kings held life-or-
death power over all their subjects, including writers.
— Elizabethan scholar **LIMON SWANSON**

It's codswallop—"By the grace of God." No king or queen
got there by "divine right." Being a royal simply means your
ancestors killed more people than a common person's ancestors.
— UK composer **LIONEL BART** (*Oliver*)

Howard Hughes has asked me to collaborate
with him on his autobiography.
— writer **CLIFFORD IRVING** in 1971

I wouldn't lie because it's a sin.
— preacher **JIM BAKKER**, who didn't consider
plagiarism lying. He sometimes searched books and
trawled the internet for sermons to claim as his own.

My family's ordinary. I don't talk about them.
. . . People wouldn't be interested.
— **BOB HOPE**, whose two daughters (all four kids
were adopted) were out lesbians and whose gay
nephew died of AIDS. Reportedly, the egocentric
comedian didn't care to share the spotlight.

My brother said he had cancer, and my family [said] he died
of that. But it's important folks should know what's killing
who . . . 'cause we have got to do something about this,
even if one effing president after another [Reagan and Bush]
doesn't want to do anything unless he's fucking forced.
— **NELL CARTER** (*Gimme a Break*),
who announced that her gay brother died of AIDS

I have just one father. I want to make peace with him.
— singer **MARVIN GAYE**, shortly before a
fight with his father, who shot him dead

I just got off tour.

— **WHITNEY HOUSTON**, apologizing for arriving late
at a White House dinner honoring South African leader
Nelson Mandela. She'd gotten off tour four days earlier.

You won't catch us!

— **HENRI PAUL**, the chauffeur driving Princess Diana in
Paris on the night of her death in 1997 to the paparazzi
chasing them, according to the *New York Daily News*

I like all people, . . . and I want to make people
aware that the sea is wonderful, that there is more
chance to be killed by lightning than a shark.

— French oceanographer **JACQUES COUSTEAU**, who
wrote a letter, auctioned posthumously, that was blatantly
anti-Semitic and complained that Depression-era jobs were
hard to come by because Jews had taken "our" jobs

We do not hate. . . . Only Israel.

— Egypt's then-dictator **HOSNI MUBARAK**. Christians
have systematically been driven out of numerous Muslim
countries, and terrorism against Christians and churches has
been encouraged or ignored by several Muslim regimes.

Tel Aviv, the capital of Israel.

— **THE BBC'S ARABIC-LANGUAGE SERVICE**,
repeatedly, despite promising to correct the
"politicised" error. Israel's capital is Jerusalem.

I'm Jewish.

I'm not Jewish.

I believe I'm half-Jewish.

— various public statements by **CARY GRANT**

Hollywood, where the truth lies. Still. Very still.

— author **BOZE HADLEIGH**

Producer Paul Gregory held a masquerade party at his Santa
Monica house. In July 1955, *Confidential* magazine, which
was terrifying Hollywood and titillating America, published
a story about guest Robert Mitchum. It said he arrived
drunk, stripped down to his socks, smeared himself with
ketchup, then announced, "I'm a hamburger, well done."

— columnist **LEE GRAHAM**

Confidential had to water down the Mitchum story. He
didn't strip, but he did pull out his cock, placed it on a
serving plate, added catsup, and turned to Paul Gregory
and his [also gay] associate Charles Laughton, then
asked, "Which one of you wants to eat this first?"

— columnist **JAMES BACON**. The true version, with minor
variations about Mitchum's "hot dog," was also revealed in a 1988
TV documentary and the 2018 book *"Confidential" Confidential*.

Unfair! They were only giving them more of what they wanted.

— game-show panelist **PEGGY CASS** on beauty-
pageant contestants dismissed from competition
because they padded their swimsuits

This girl, single-handed, may make bosoms a thing of the past.

— director **BILLY WILDER** on then-new
screen superstar Audrey Hepburn

She was so full of evil that one day her head
just popped off and exploded.

— **MAE WEST**, abetting the misconception that Jayne
Mansfield was decapitated during her fatal car accident. Only
her wig came off. West hated the younger blonde because
Mickey Hargitay, the chief muscleman in Mae's nightclub
act, very publicly courted and then wed Mansfield.

I love and treasure women.

— **GEORGE C. SCOTT**, who violently abused, among
others, costar Ava Gardner and wife Colleen Dewhurst. In
later years, he was still coming on to women a third his age,
some of whom threatened suit for sexual harassment.

Numerous biographers have claimed Thomas
Jefferson had no children by his slave Sally Hemings.
. . . In 1998, DNA proved the claim false.

— actor **LON JEFFERS**, who portrayed Jefferson for public
schools. Jefferson commenced sexual relations with Hemings
when he was 44 and she was 14. Her consent was not required.

When I played President Grover Cleveland.

— **RONALD REAGAN**, who didn't play the
19th-century president but rather baseball player
Grover Cleveland Alexander in the 1952 film *The
Winning Team* (more likely forgetfulness than a lie)

There is no Soviet domination of Eastern Europe, and there never will be under a Ford administration.

— President **GERALD FORD** in 1976
(more likely dumbness than a lie)

✳

I came right out and asked [the president] why he had homosexuals on his senior staff at the White House.

— preacher **JERRY FALWELL** at a conservative Alaska election gathering. White House transcripts later proved no such question was asked.

✳

I did it for commercial purposes.

— **DAVID BOWIE**, explaining away why he'd come out of the closet. In the more conservative 1980s, he went back in.

She and I . . . just drifted apart.

— **LAURENCE OLIVIER** on actress and first wife Jill Esmond, better known than he when they married. The lesbian actress left the bisexual actor for another woman, and they moved to Wimbledon.

✳

My second marriage is turning out to be happier.

— **VIVIAN VANCE** (*I Love Lucy*). Almost certainly it was her happiest, but it was her fourth. Vance kept mum about her first two. Her third was to actor Phil Ober, a wife beater. Her final marriage was to John Dodds, a gay publisher.

Roy and I are just good friends. . . . The [tigers] are like our children.

— **SIEGFRIED FISCHBACHER** of longtime couple Siegfried and Roy

We are the best of friends. Period.

— semi-out gay author **GORE VIDAL** on Howard Austen, his partner of 53 years

He's still in [the closet], still hopelessly ambitious. . . . He participated in a mock wedding ceremony with a platonic friend so non–fact checkers like the tabloids can say he's been married—to a woman.

— UK writer **KEN FERGUSON** on Paul Reubens, a.k.a. Pee-wee Herman

I went to live with him when I was 12.

— **RICHARD BURTON**, born Richard Jenkins, on moving in with gay instructor Philip Burton, whose surname he took. The future actor moved in at 17 but gave the younger age to lend the relationship a platonic gloss. Philip Burton outlived Richard and was included in the star's will.

I'm three-quarters Irish and a quarter Mexican and proud of it.

— two-time Oscar-winner **ANTHONY QUINN**, three-quarters Mexican and a quarter Irish

He's as Irish as you or me.

— **RAQUEL WELCH**, whose first husband was Patrick Welch. For decades her publicity avoided that her father was Bolivian and her last name was Tejada.

✳

Debbie Reynolds upset millions statewide in 1991 when she opined that Latinas [should] have fewer kids, collect less welfare, . . . and go to work. . . . [In] fact, Hispanics receive considerably less welfare than other groups and are among the hardest-working people in California, propping up its economy while often underpaid and underserviced.

— from the book **MEXICO'S MOST WANTED**

✳

I love Albuquerque, New Mexico, where I was born and reared.

— **VIVIAN VANCE** (Ethel Mertz on *I Love Lucy*) disliked her real home state and later said, "Dorothy in *The Wizard of Oz* was so happy to wake up in Kansas. Not I! I'd have looked for another cyclone and stood right in its path!"

✳

I will never do another TV series. It couldn't top *I Love Lucy*, and I'd be foolish to try. In this business, you have to know when to get off.

— **LUCILLE BALL** in 1960. She did three more series, the last one a disaster.

✳

Miss Angela Lansbury was our first and only choice to portray Jessica Fletcher.

— **PRESS RELEASE FOR THE TV SERIES *MURDER, SHE WROTE***, which was first offered to Doris Day, then to Jean Stapleton (of *All in the Family*)

October 31 (1902)

— **UNIVERSAL'S REVISED BIRTHDAY** for Elsa Lanchester, who enacted *The Bride of Frankenstein* in 1935. Born on October 28, she resented the natal repositioning to a scarier date.

✳

I knew Bob. He chose to lie. . . . As Turner Classic Movies' host, he said William Haines quit being a movie star to become a decorator. There was reaction, so Bob had to retract it.

— columnist **GEORGE CHRISTY** on secretly gay TCM host Robert Osborne. Haines, caught in the 1930s with a serviceman in his room at the YMCA, was fired by MGM and blackballed by the other studios.

✳

I knew Peter [Bogdanovich] when he was a writer who wanted to make movies. . . . I found him a terrific novel called *Midnight Cowboy*. He promised if it got made, I'd play Ratso Rizzo—a natural for me, Italian American. When he couldn't get it made, he promised me a lead role in something else. I discovered he'd interviewed other actors about playing Ratso. He lied to me. And of course he never gave me any role. . . . Peter was willing to lend a helping hand—to those above him.

— **SAL MINEO** (*Rebel without a Cause*)

✳

Michelangelo designed the colorful costumes worn by the Vatican's Swiss Guard.

— **SEVERAL TOURIST BROCHURES AND BOOKS**. The costumes were designed in 1914. The Vatican, located inside Rome, is the world's smallest country, population about 800, all male. It has its own currency, stamps, newspapers, and the Bank of the Holy Ghost.

Italian cuisine hasn't much changed since the Romans.
. . . They even had *lasanum*, a precursor to lasagna.
— food writer **KATHLEEN GIBSON**. Try to imagine
Italian cuisine, including lasagna, without tomato
sauce. Tomatoes come from South America and
weren't imported into Europe until the 1500s.

Margarine is a healthier alternative to butter.
— anti-butter crusader Dr. **ANCEL KEYS**

The dimple machine's face-fitting spring will provide a fine set
of dimples as its two tiny knobs press into the cheeks over time.
— 1936 promotion by **ISABELLA GILBERT** of Rochester,
New York. No such machine could produce dimples, but
today a surgeon can, via a 20-minute operation done
from inside the mouth, involving a cheek muscle.

It is anti-French, . . . a lie, as if we speak vulgarly.
Whenever in English they say, "Pardon my
French," they mean dirty *English* words!
— French actress **DELPHINE SEYRIG**

Yes, I am a prude!
— **KATHARINE HEPBURN**, who in 1969 was
reportedly the first star to utter a four-letter word
("Shit!") on Broadway, in the musical *Coco*

Michelangelo's *David* is excessively realistic.

— writer/editor **DONALD RAWLEY**, objecting to the fig-leaf-free statue. The above is an opinion (prudish), but the statue, possibly the world's most famous, is not realistic. Though the Renaissance was a step forward artistically and socially, it wasn't enough so to depict the Jewish king as circumcised.

Pravda

— **THE OFFICIAL NEWSPAPER OF THE SOVIET UNION**. Its name means *truth*.

✳

Yes, Virginia, there really is a Santa Claus.

— ***NEW YORK SUN*** in 1897

✳

The first time you hear a rumor, you don't believe it. The second time you hear a rumor, you don't believe it. The third time you hear a rumor, you believe it.

— **CHINESE PROVERB**

✳

Mrs. [Eleanor] Roosevelt and Miss [Lorena] Hickok were just good friends. . . . Those are only rumors.

— US history teacher **WILBUR STALEY**. Publication of the women's correspondence made clear they were in love.

✳

Let's say prevaricating. It sounds classier than lying.

— **CAROLYN JONES** (*The Addams Family*)

Let's not call it blackmail. Just call it a vicious threat.
— comedian **PAUL LYNDE**

✳

Sarcasm is the shallow end of lying.
— comedian **SOUPY SALES**

✳

Honesty is the best image.
— billionaire and MGM owner **KIRK KERKORIAN**

✳

Those who know the truth are not equal to those who love it.
— **KONG QIU** (Confucius)

✳

A half-truth is also a half-lie.
— writer and Nobel laureate **YASUNARI KAWABATA**

✳

Big lies are told by those with large political or financial
ambitions. Small lies are told for short-term benefits
and are sometimes known as good manners.
— social critic **QUENTIN CRISP**

11

Costars and Peers

You'd better answer that. It could be somebody important.

— **ELIZABETH II** to a girl invited to a party for young achievers at Buckingham Palace during the Queen's Golden Jubilee celebrations in 2002. While chatting with the monarch, the girl's cell phone rang. Mortified, she froze until Her Majesty urged her to answer the call.

I knew Doris Day before she was a virgin.

— **OSCAR LEVANT**, who costarred in Day's first film. She was Hollywood's biggest box-office actress.

I don't dislike her. I dislike her reveling in furs, as if they enhance her and don't involve the torture and killing of animals. She has little conscience. . . . No further comment.

— **DORIS DAY** on Ivana Trump

I may be my own worst enemy.

— **PETER SELLERS**. "Not while I'm alive," replied director Billy Wilder. Sellers pulled out of a Wilder film at the last minute.

I'm glad [James] Dean's dead. It makes more room for me.

— **STEVE MCQUEEN** to fellow actor John Gilmore

Rock, Rory, Tab and Troy, and Guy and Rip? These stars' made-up names are the most memorable thing about them.

— *Tonight Show* host **JACK PAAR**

There are no heroes today. Name *one*. Michael Jackson?
— **BETTE DAVIS**

✳

He's a tyrant, and I don't like him!
— **FRANCES BAVIER** (Aunt Bee on *The Andy Griffith Show*) on Andy Griffith

✳

Lucille Ball was a control freak. Had to be in charge of everything. Never saw a woman who took her comedy so seriously.
— **PHYLLIS DILLER**

✳

I commented on the surprising fact that this gentleman 22 years my senior was going to play my husband. He overheard me, and his one-sided feud was on. . . . Eventually we were offered our own spin-off series, for very good money, . . . being the stars, not the featured players. Bill's life was booze, baseball, and money. He never forgave me for saying no. But a king's ransom couldn't have induced me to continue working with that awful old so-and-so.
— **VIVIAN VANCE** on *I Love Lucy* costar William Frawley

✳

He lost out on movie immortality when he was replaced as the Tin Man in *The Wizard of Oz*. . . . Decades later, he experienced TV success with *The Beverly Hillbillies*. . . . He has not lost his bitterness and basic dissatisfaction.
— **NANCY KULP** (Jane Hathaway) on costar Buddy Ebsen

There was doubt about the Spock character . . . intended as a satellite to the captain character. . . . But fan mail for Mr. Spock kept coming in, steadily, increasingly. People were so intrigued by the concept of him. And perhaps a little by the way I played him. . . . So it became Captain Kirk *and* Mr. Spock. . . . Mr. Spock was not a passing fancy.
— *Star Trek* costar **LEONARD NIMOY**

Mary Tyler Moore wasn't Mary Richards [her series character]. . . . Her parents were alcoholics, and she admitted she was a harsh mother to her son, who died young. . . . She turned down *Mary and Rhoda* after learning Valerie Harper would get as big a salary as hers. She finally gave in because by then Mary was washed up on TV.
— columnist **GEORGE CHRISTY**. The telefilm didn't lead to the hoped-for series.

Classy as hell but one of the all-time Hollywood dykes.
— **PAUL LYNDE** on *Bewitched* costar Agnes Moorehead

*

The rumor is that Jonathan Frid, who played Barnabas Collins on *Dark Shadows*, was paid *not* to come out of the closet . . . via a generous annual stipend, allegedly from Dan Curtis, the show's creator and producer. Barnabas, a vampire, was a romantic sex symbol. . . . Frid's coming out would have hurt sales of the DVDs and other *Dark Shadows* merchandise that fans still buy.
— *Scarlet Street* magazine publisher **RICHARD VALLEY**

Merv Griffin was fat, no sex symbol, filthy rich, his own boss. But he hated being nicknamed Merv the Perv. . . . It encouraged him to stay closeted and pretend-date Eva Gabor.

— comedian **RIP TAYLOR**

✳

If Barbara Walters advanced the cause of women in electronic journalism, and she did, it was coincidental. She's a barracuda. . . . She's cozied up to powerful men, including dictators, . . . and she was the beard for Roy Cohn, the most hated attorney of the 20th century. She appeared as a character witness at Cohn's 1986 disbarment hearing, and of course he was disbarred.

— southern California news anchor **CHRIS BURROUS**

✳

Michael Landon. A true-blue phony. I did a telethon with him and was astonished by his rudeness to the noncelebrity telephone volunteers. He wouldn't sign autographs, would not shake hands—he backed off and refused—wouldn't even smile.

— **PHIL CAREY**, most widely known for Granny Goose potato chip commercials

✳

I used to get a kick out of little Robert Clary telling me the latest about his "son." His stepson. Robert didn't romanticize his marriage because he knew I knew it was a marriage of convenience, as they say. . . . His wife's son was by her previous husband. That relationship was not felicitous. By another token, her marriage of friendship to a, let's face it, very nice homosexual man, was happy, and it lasted.

— *Hogan's Heroes* costar (and later *Family Feud* host) **RICHARD DAWSON**

Dan Rowan, . . . I'd rather talk about Dick Martin. Dick was fun. He didn't take it too seriously. . . . Dan was a shit. I'm not alone in this view—ask around.

— **ARTE JOHNSON** of *Rowan and Martin's Laugh-In*

The biggest men in Tinseltown were, reputedly, Milton Berle and Forrest Tucker. When we did *F Troop*, I teased Forrest, asked him to show it, to prove the legend. But he was shy. . . . One day, with urgent news, I rushed in to his dressing room without knocking. All I can say is: Wow. And wow. The legend was true. . . . Guy could have earned even more as a porn star.

— costar **LARRY STORCH**

Before *Golden Girls*, I worked with Bea Arthur and Betty White separately. People assume Bea is lots tougher than Betty. But our Rose Nyland isn't Betty. Neither was Sue Ann Nivens on *Mary Tyler Moore*. Betty's current image would be quite different if Sue Ann had come after Rose. . . . Actresses *act*.

— **RUE MCCLANAHAN** (Blanche on *The Golden Girls*)

Is she the one and only new star out of the mid-1970s? . . . I'm so tired of seeing Farrah Fawcett-Majors everywhere, she of major hair and poster-deep talent.

— Broadway star **GRETCHEN WYLER**

Farrah said Raquel Welch treated her badly on *Myra Breckinridge*.
But then, Raquel said Mae West, who was top-billed, treated
her badly. So it goes. . . . Older resents younger, uses her
clout. The difference is, Raquel and Farrah had a love scene
together. Guess it didn't thaw into warm feelings. Or did it?

— Hollywood biographer **JOE MORELLA**

This may not see print, but Raquel Welch is a bitch on
wheels. She came from nothing, was proclaimed the sexiest
woman since Marilyn Monroe, and treats everyone badly. But
don't think it hasn't hurt her career, now she's over 40.

— *Hollywood Babylon* author **KENNETH ANGER**

Bob Hope is a barely funny, very selfish reactionary and user.
He used patriotism and the troops overseas for publicity.

— MYRNA LOY

Bob Hope is an applause junkie. Instead of growing old gracefully
or doing something with his money, all he does is have an
anniversary, with the president looking on. He's a pathetic guy.

— MARLON BRANDO

Jerry Lewis takes criticism much too personally.
He explodes, then he stews, then he explodes
again. It's as if to criticize him is treason.

— DEAN MARTIN, Lewis's former showbiz partner

I've read that Dirk Bogarde's cruel streak can be attributed
to his fight for acceptance as an actor, as a homosexual
man, and as a writer. And all the time I thought it
was just because he's quite an unpleasant fellow.
— UK actor and costar **MICHAEL HORDERN**

John Huston was comfortable working with openly gay men
like Truman Capote and Tennessee Williams but uncomfortable
with secretly gay men like Montgomery Clift. Not because he
admired honesty. Because the closeted ones were more average
and could *pass*, . . . that threatened Huston and made him hostile.
— gay producer **ISMAIL MERCHANT**

Raquel Welch hates me ever since we did *100 Rifles* [1968].
. . . One day she said, "Why haven't you made a pass
at me?" Without the slightest pause I replied, "Because
I'm positive that I'd pull up your dress, pull down your
panties, and find an 8 × 10 glossy of your cunt."
— BURT REYNOLDS

She projects the passion of a Good Humor ice
cream: frozen, on a stick, and all vanilla.
— SPENCER TRACY on actress Nancy
Davis (later Nancy Reagan)

I found out Carole [Lombard] wasn't a natural blonde.
We're in her dressing room, talking. She starts undressing.
I didn't know what to do. . . . She's talking away and
mixing peroxide and some other liquid in a bowl.
With a piece of cotton, she begins to apply the liquid
to dye the hair around her honeypot. She glanced up
and saw my amazed look and smiled. "Relax, Georgie,
I'm just making my collar and cuffs match."

— fellow movie star **GEORGE RAFT**

✳

James Mason wore a false torso beneath his shirt. It
enlarged his chest, making him more intense and
virile. . . . He wasn't at all self-conscious about being
strapped into it on the set in front of everybody.

— screenwriter **ARTHUR LAURENTS**

✳

Then there was *Queen Bee* [1955], a Joan Crawford soap.
She wrote me a welcoming note saying how she'd always
admired veterans of the silent days. I never had the courage
to inform her I was actually a year younger than she was.
On every Crawford picture, she had a younger cast
member to berate, and on this one, when she had to
slap pretty little Lucy Marlowe, she did so with such
fury it could be heard all over the sound stage.

— **FAY WRAY** (*King Kong*)

I was a teenage star in Disney movies. Then a boy I fooled around with told his mother, who told Walt Disney, who told me I better start liking girls, fast. . . . My option at Disney wasn't renewed, but Walt let me return to the studio to do the final Merlin Jones movie because those were big moneymakers for him.

— **TOMMY KIRK** (Old Yeller)

He liked to be known as Uncle Walt. Liked being dictator of his world of Disney. Liked getting credit, for most everything, . . . certainly liked money.

— **ED WYNN** (Uncle Albert in Mary Poppins)

I worked for Disney and was glad to leave, as many did. . . . I won't say he was specifically anti-Mexican; he was more equal-opportunity bigoted. . . . He did not like unions and didn't make his mouse factory overly pleasant to work in.

— multi-Emmy-Award-winning animator **BILL MELENDEZ**, who brought Peanuts to television

It does make it easier if you dislike the actor playing a character you're supposed to dislike. Richard Crenna [in Body Heat] made it very easy. A big mouth, inappropriately and unprofessionally airing ugly opinions any time he so wished.

— **WILLIAM HURT**

It doesn't compute that with all his success—the singing and
the movies—Frank Sinatra was so moody and touchy, . . .
vindictive, with a gangster mentality. He enjoyed the company
of hoods and sometimes had them beat up people for him. Or
did it himself. He did it to me. He thought it was funny.

— producer-turned-writer **DOMINICK DUNNE**

I fall in love with all the actors in my films. They
are the prolongation of my penis. Yes, my penis,
like Pinocchio's nose, my penis grows!

— bisexual director **BERNARDO BERTOLUCCI**

Pinocchio's nose grew, but with Michael Jackson, the
bigger the lies, the smaller his nose. The *New York Post*
reported he's had six nose jobs. It's freakish. . . . Speaking
of which, how to explain [his] wanting to buy the bones of
the Elephant Man? Empathy? Freak solidarity? What?

— librarian and editor **LEONARD KNIFFEL**

Elizabeth Taylor and Michael Jackson . . . were closer friends in
public. He showered her with expensive gifts, partly to retain
her friendship. She gave him respectability, which he sorely
needed, with all those pedophilia charges. And he gave Liz, in
the twilight of her career, publicity and made her seem hip.

— **JOE HYAMS**, publicist (45 years at Warner Bros.)

There's so damn few positive black gay role models. . . .
All these closeted actors like Paul Winfield and Sherman
Hemsley [*The Jeffersons*] and all the ones on the down-low.
It's a crime they don't at some point come out, 'cause young
gay black males are the most vulnerable of all to AIDS.
— African American writer **E. LYNN HARRIS**

Luther Vandross stayed in the closet for his mother.
. . . He was afraid his lady fans would be disappointed.
. . . Must've had a hard time with his being gay.
— singer **LOU RAWLS**. Not as hard as members of the
black LGBTQ community who lack fame and fortune.

I asked if he ever thought about coming out of the closet,
as more actors were doing. He said by not getting married,
that's already the showbiz equivalent to being out. What
I think he also felt was, he's already one visible minority;
it's still more difficult being known as two minorities.
— **RON CAREY** on *Barney Miller* costar Ron Glass

I'll tell a tale on myself now. I'm wildly attracted to women.
But I can understand why at given moments someone might
think I'm homosexual. . . . When I'm with a homosexual,
I get a little homosexual. To make them feel at home,
you see? I kind of camp a little. To bring them out. So
they won't feel like they're with a terrible straight.
— ORSON WELLES

Cheetah bit me whenever he could. The [Tarzan] apes were all homosexuals, eager to wrap their paws around Johnny Weissmuller's thighs. They were jealous of me, and I loathed them.
— **MAUREEN "JANE" O'SULLIVAN** (mother of Mia Farrow)

✴

Among other things, I did Tarzan movies. Give me an actor like Johnny Weissmuller anytime. If I saw Weissmuller scratching his groin, I knew either his loincloth was too tight or he was pulling at his foreskin. A very uncomplicated actor.
— director **RICHARD THORPE**

✴

[Sean Connery] is a big Easter Island statue, he's so damned old! At least make him pollinate with someone who's still young enough to be his daughter, but no! They have to have someone who's his great-granddaughter! Big fat fossil fuel—you're doing love scenes! Just let him pump gas!
— comedienne-accordionist **JUDY TENUTA**

✴

Thank you, Mr. Falk, but for the same money
I can get an actor with two eyes.
— Columbia studio head **HARRY COHN** to aspiring (Jewish) actor Peter Falk, who lost his right eye at age three and did a screen test to reassure Cohn

✴

My plump little hunchback.
— MGM chief **LOUIS B. MAYER**'s nickname for a young, insecure Judy Garland

I have just come from the Actors Studio where I saw
Marilyn Monroe. She had no girdle on. Her ass was
hanging out. She is a disgrace to the industry.
— **JOAN CRAWFORD** in 1955

✳

Joan Crawford—Hollywood's first case of
syphilis. . . . I wouldn't sit on her toilet!
— **BETTE DAVIS** on her rival, who began in silent movies

✳

Poor, old, rotten-egg Joan. I kept my mouth shut about
her for nearly a quarter of a century, but she was a mean,
tipsy, powerful, rotten-egg lady. I'm still not going to tell
what she did to me [shooting *Johnny Guitar*, 1954].
Other people have written some of it, but they don't know it
all, and they never will because I am a very nice person and I
don't like to talk about the dead, even if they were rotten eggs.
— **MERCEDES MCCAMBRIDGE** (the voice
of the devil in *The Exorcist*) in her memoirs

✳

Black media figures like Whitney Houston and Michael Jackson
need a history lesson. They blithely diss Jews, displaying prejudice
and ignorance. For over a century in the US, the one white
group to consistently support blacks' civil rights were the Jews.
And their worst enemies were radical Christian groups
like the Ku Klux Klan, which also hated Jews.
— publicist **HOWARD BRAGMAN**

Elizabeth Taylor was turned down by several stars she invited
to attend the first big AIDS fundraiser. . . . Frank Sinatra
said he didn't want to be involved with a "fag disease." The
press was reporting AIDS as if it were a gay disease started
by promiscuous male flight attendants. We now know it
originated in Africa and that 70 percent of its victims,
mostly in Third World nations, are heterosexuals.

— actor **ALEXIS ARQUETTE**

✳

My definition of ridiculous? One is "a closeted fashion designer."
In Europe most of us are out. In the USA, many or most are
inside. Some do come out, after the wrinkles appear. . . . If one
is embarrassed, why become a fashion designer? Drive a truck!

— designer **KARL LAGERFELD**

✳

I was asked to play James Bond in the first 007 picture but
declined, being under contract to MGM. Ironically, MGM
eventually amalgamated with United Artists. . . . They got
around to choosing Sean Connery, who was all wrong for the
part. He brought in humor and irony. [Novelist] Ian Fleming
had no humor. But the masses didn't know Fleming's Bond.
They came to know Connery's Bond, and he made it a hit.

— UK actor **RICHARD JOHNSON**

Adam West fell violently in love with himself when his show
became a ratings smash and was broadcast twice a week. He
thought he was a world-class star and later asserted he'd been
offered but declined the film role of James Bond. Jim Bond, . . .
an American 007? Totally false. Bond's producers would never
hire an actor whose fame was tied to a comic-strip character.
— casting director/producer **RENEE VALENTE** on TV's *Batman*

I saw him close-up in a drug-inspired rage, and it
was frightening. He was verging toward violence
but managed, barely, to control himself. . . . I'm not
antidrugs per se, but drugs can be the unholy Satan.
— singer **SINÉAD O'CONNOR** on singer Prince

I met Patricia Highsmith in the late 1960s. . . . She, I, and
a mutual friend spent an interesting afternoon. Two things
struck me: Pat admitted she was crime-prone and positive
she'd have been a criminal if she didn't write about crime—
her protagonists, you know, aren't heroes but killers.
And she was blatantly against Jews. Gave no reason. I
mean there's no legitimate reason, but she had a mental
thing against them that grew worse as she aged.
— UK writer **SHIRLEY DU BOULAY**

When Hitchcock filmed *Strangers on a Train*, it escalated Patricia Highsmith's profile. She didn't complain publicly that in the movie, only the villain committed murder. In her novel, both men kill someone. She was very upset about the liberty taken with her plot but also very glad to take the movie-rights money.
— literary agent **JIM PINKSTON**

✳

Kate Hepburn was bi or lesbian. Did she have an affair with Howard Hughes, or did he fly to the *Sylvia Scarlett* location to visit her costar and his chum or boyfriend Cary Grant? There are several indications that Hughes went both ways. . . . He was associated with more beautiful actresses than any other man, but most have gone on record saying it was all business and he never slept with them.
— writer/producer **ROBERT S. LEVINSON**

✳

She is humorless and uncomfortable being a woman.
— playwright and screenwriter **ARTHUR LAURENTS** on Katharine Hepburn, with whom he worked and played tennis

✳

The most devastating event in Katharine Hepburn's life was the teenaged suicide of her older brother Tom, her role model and closest friend. Relatives said she never got over it. She seemingly blamed the suicide on his homosexuality rather than the homophobia that may have driven him to it. . . . In later years, she privately admitted Tom was gay.
— **GORE VIDAL**. Until quite late in life, Hepburn gave out Tom's birthdate as her own.

I was a fan of *Friends* till it kept on trying to make jokes out of "You mean he's really not gay?" situations. The policy on Matthew Perry's Chandler character was "write it gay but play it straight," a cowardly cop-out. . . . Matthew has publicly dated some high-profile women and once got engaged, then unengaged. I'm not going to be the one to tell all. "Play it straight," that's all I'll say.

— **CRAIG ZADAN**, writer/producer (*Chicago*)

＊

It's a shame to hide our wonderful background, . . . but the prejudice. We are Mexican, but my last name is Day, and my brother is the movie star Gilbert Roland.

— assistant director (*The Ten Commandments; Hello, Dolly!*) **CHICO DAY**, born Francisco Alonso

＊

I didn't have much choice, covering up. Everyone knows US citizens of Japanese origin were rounded up and illegally put into camps during World War II. They didn't do that to citizens of German origin. . . . My last name was Suzuki. I changed it to Soo, a Chinese name. To Caucasians, Chinese and Japanese look alike. But so do Germans and Poles and French, and they were all enemies then.

— **JACK SOO** (*Barney Miller*)

＊

I always thought he was toward the fascist side. But Franco Zeffirelli sued some Italian periodical that called him fascist, and he won. Didn't change my mind. A talented gay director but a creep. . . . One of his publicized opinions was, if a woman chooses abortion, she should be executed. That ain't fascist?

— **VAL BISOGLIO** (*Saturday Night Fever*)

Ginger Rogers was one of the worst, red-baiting,
terrifying reactionaries in Hollywood.
— blacklisted director **JOSEPH LOSEY**, who
had to move to Britain to find work

✳

Hedda Hopper was a cheerleader for McCarthy's witch hunters.
. . . She hated that Kennedy, a Democrat and a Catholic, got into
office . . . and had the nerve to criticize the president in print
for going to see *Spartacus*, which gave actual credit to a formerly
blacklisted screenwriter. . . . JFK helped to end the blacklist.
— *Spartacus* star and coproducer **KIRK DOUGLAS**
on the powerful gossip columnist

✳

Self-worship was Hedda Hopper's approach. Her living room had
a shrine centered on a magazine cover of Hedda, framed in real
gold, she said. The cover was blown up to worship size, and there
were even votive candles flanking the holy likeness of St. Hedda,
whose favorite pastimes were her cocktail bar, going to the races,
and trying to crucify anyone who crossed her or she didn't like.
— **LEW AYRES**, best known for the Dr. Kildare movies

✳

It's a grand irony that Hedda Hopper's only child was gay
actor William Hopper. It was whispered he and Raymond
Burr on *Perry Mason* were an item. . . . Hedda tried to out
various male stars and was sued by Stewart Granger. She
despised Cary Grant, but he was too big for her to harm
him; the studios protected their biggest investments.
— film historian **CARLOS CLARENS**

Barbara Stanwyck.

— **PAUL LYNDE**'s answer to the *Hollywood Squares* question "Who was known as Old Blood and Guts?"

She stole that part from me. . . . I campaigned for it, tested for it, got it, my wardrobe was completed. Then [Barbara] Stanwyck, who'd already turned down the part, suddenly decided she wanted it. She was a bigger star, so the studio gave it to her. I know she only chose to do it because I'd said yes. What she had against me, I don't know. She wasn't very nice.

— **LUCILLE BALL**. Stanwyck received an Oscar nomination for the 1941 hit *Ball of Fire.*

I was visiting Italy some time after Gore Vidal moved there, and eventually we connected on the telephone. He called me to say, "I passed by your hotel yesterday." I was perfectly candid and said, "Thank you so much."

— rival writer **TRUMAN CAPOTE**

By their position in the family, elders are typically more duty-bound than their younger siblings. . . . Princess Margaret was to the queen as Billy Carter was to President Carter.

— UK writer **GIL GIBSON**

I think you are wonderful and charming, and if I should ever change from liking girls better, you would be my first thought.

— **HUMPHREY BOGART** (star of *Beat the Devil*, 1954, which Truman Capote scripted) to the young gay writer

Dear 338171, May I call you 338?

— **NOËL COWARD**, attempting to pry open
the closet of T. E. Lawrence (of Arabia), who used
numerals in his personal correspondence

In the 1940s, an actress tried to out a rising gay actor. . . .
The actor [lied] to his studio head, who told other studio
heads that the actress invented the story because he'd
raped her. Rape was less likely to end the actor's career.

— historian/publisher **MARTIN GREIF**

It never hit the press. They shield Michael Jackson because they
shield gay guys but also because he's black . . . *was?* Anyway,
he had a blond boyfriend before solo stardom. When father
Joseph found out, he hit the roof, put a stop to that! Michael
always feared him. . . . He avoided him as much as he could.

— African American singer **SYLVESTER**

Michael wasn't thrilled to be a boy. . . . He'd rather have
been a beautiful white female. He said so more than
once. But all that plastic surgery? That's because he was
trying to look as unlike his father, Joe, as possible.

— African American poet **ESSEX HEMPHILL**

Yes, I learned that Andy Warhol did cum facials, using his own. I
don't know if they worked, but it was a clever way of recycling.

— stage and TV actor **MICHAEL JETER**

I wasn't there, but part of *The Man Who Would Be King* was shot near the Sahara. At night the women were confined at home, but the village men could go to the disco, . . . more for the drinks than the dancing. Sean [Connery] told me that one night he felt like dancing, but he didn't want to ask his driver, who was too ugly. So he asked to borrow another actor's driver.

— **CHRISTOPHER PLUMMER**, who played
author Rudyard Kipling in the film

Mickey Rooney was on some talk show. The host asked about gay actors. Rooney said when he was a star there were no gay actors. The host mentioned Cary Grant.

Rooney said, "He's about as gay as my left foot."

Actress Gloria De Haven, sitting next to him, said, "Mickey, I didn't know you had a gay left foot."

— **TOMMY KIRK** (*The Absent-Minded Professor*)

I remember Tallulah [Bankhead] telling of going into a public ladies' room and discovering there was no toilet tissue. She looked underneath the booth and said to the lady in the next stall, "I beg your pardon, do you happen to have any toilet tissue in there?" The lady said no.

So Tallulah said, "Well, then, dahling, do you have two fives for a ten?"

— **ETHEL MERMAN**

12

■ ■ ■ ■ ■ ■ ■ ■ ■

Critic-sizing

I read the book, I read the script, I saw the
movie, and I still don't understand it.
— **SEAN CONNERY** on *The Lord of the Rings*

✳

This is not a novel to be tossed aside lightly.
It should be thrown with great force.
— **DOROTHY PARKER**

✳

For those who missed it the first time, this is your
golden opportunity: you can miss it again.
— UK actor **MICHAEL BILLINGTON** on the revival of *Godspell*

✳

Now, scenery is bigger and stars are smaller. The
chandelier in *Phantom [of the Opera]* and the staircase
in *Sunset Boulevard* should get billing.
— **BEA ARTHUR**, who switched from theater to television

✳

A farce or a comedy is best played. A tragedy is best read at home.
— **ABRAHAM LINCOLN** in 1863 after a performance
of *The Merchant of Venice* starring Edwin Booth.
Two years later, he was assassinated by Booth's
younger brother while attending a comedy.

✳

We fancy that any real child might be more puzzled
than enchanted by this stiff, overwrought story.
— 1865 **CHILDREN'S BOOKS REVIEW** of
Lewis Carroll's *Alice in Wonderland*

Interesting that our number 1 children's author isn't a parent. . . . His child must dwell within.
— novelist **LEON URIS** on Theodor Geisel, a.k.a. Dr. Seuss

✳

What sadist placed it high on a bough, so when the wind blows and it breaks, "down will come baby, cradle and all"? I ask you!
— author **HELENE HANFF**. The nursery rhyme/song dates back to at least 1765 and *Mother Goose's Melody Book*.

✳

"Write about what you *know*" is for children. Rodgers and Hammerstein never visited Oklahoma or Thailand yet wrote those wondrous musicals *Oklahoma!* and *The King and I*. . . . For adults, it's "Write about what *interests* you."
— Broadway star **CAROL CHANNING**

✳

The girl doesn't, it seems to me, have a special perception or feeling which would lift that book above the "curiosity" level.
— **PUBLISHER'S REJECTION LETTER**
in 1952 of the diary of Anne Frank

✳

Anyone who sees and paints a sky green and pastures blue ought to be sterilized.
— former housepainter **ADOLF HITLER** on modern art

✳

When I asked my first husband if he liked painting, he said he generally preferred wallpaper.
— **JOAN RIVERS**

Gone with the Wind is going to be the
biggest flop in Hollywood history.

— **GARY COOPER** in 1937, after declining to
star in the screen version of the best-seller

✳

I can't imagine Rhett Butler chasing you for 10 years.

— *GWTW* producer **DAVID O. SELZNICK** rejecting
Katharine Hepburn as Scarlett O'Hara

✳

It's pretty thin, son. I don't think people will follow it.

— **HENRY FONDA** to son Peter on his movie
Easy Rider, which became a huge hit

✳

I wouldn't read a book titled *Chesapeake*. One reviewer said
it's a page-turner. If it is, I'll bet not all the pages get read.

— **TRUMAN CAPOTE** on James Michener's novel

✳

The covers of this book are too far apart.

— writer **AMBROSE BIERCE**

✳

It is claimed that everyone has a book in them. . . . In
the majority of cases, that is where it should remain.

— actress/politician **GLENDA JACKSON**,
when asked about writing her memoirs

✳

Get rid of the pointed-ears guy.

— **AN NBC EXECUTIVE** to *Star Trek* creator Gene
Roddenberry in 1966 on the Mr. Spock character

I quit watching *The Match Game* because of that bitter drunk, the butt-right-in panelist Brett Somers, who had diarrhea of the mouth.
— columnist **LEE GRAHAM**

✳

Bob Barker is excellent on animal rights, but he's also what #MeToo is about. . . . Some men who love animals don't much like people, especially women.
— screenwriter **HARRIET FRANK** (*Norma Rae, Hud*) to *Pet Press* in 2019

✳

The Lawrence Welk Show: good music badly performed.
— **GLENN HUGHES** of the Village People

✳

Olivia Newton-John is Australia's gift to insomniacs. It's the blonde singing the bland.
— African American singer **MINNIE RIPERTON**

✳

I loved that song "The Way We Were." Now sometimes it haunts me, . . . ever since I heard Aretha Franklin sing it on the Grammys. She murdered it.
— celebrity impressionist **JIM BAILEY**

✳

Wagner's music is better than it sounds.
— **MARK TWAIN**

The bagpipes sound exactly the same when you have finished learning them as when you start.

— conductor Sir **THOMAS BEECHAM**

✳

Far too noisy, my dear Mozart. Far too many notes.

— Austrian emperor **JOSEF II** in 1786, after attending the first performance of Mozart's opera *The Marriage of Figaro*

✳

People are wrong when they say opera is not what it used to be. It is what it used to be. That is what's wrong with it.

— **NOËL COWARD**

✳

If a thing isn't worth saying, you sing it.

— 18th-century French polymath **PIERRE BEAUMARCHAIS** on opera

✳

FIRST OPERA SINGER: Did you know I insured my voice for half a million dollars?

SECOND OPERA SINGER: Excellent! And what did you do with the money?

✳

I expected the suicide of Elvis Presley's only grandson to draw more media coverage. One reason it didn't was the boy's anticharisma. . . . There was nothing there. What Elvis had that made him a megastar died with Elvis. No part was passed on to any relative.

— showbiz columnist **NIKKI FINKE**

Anne Heche came from an extremely dysfunctional family. . . . She accurately titled her memoirs *Call Me Crazy*. . . . She died a horrible death after driving madly and recklessly, . . . blithely endangering other people's lives.

— writer **MIRIAM CASTLE**

✳

Rush Limbaugh Is a Big Fat Idiot and Other Observations

— 1996 **NONFICTION BOOK TITLE**

✳

Ten Little Niggers

— **AGATHA CHRISTIE NOVEL** later titled *Ten Little Indians* and *And Then There Were None*

✳

I have enjoyed her novels but not her assorted bigotries. . . . Christie was persistently anti-Jewish. Even after the Holocaust, she inserted viciously negative Jewish stereotypes among her characters. . . . She is a disgrace.

— Jewish UK actress **JOAN GREENWOOD**

✳

You can't accept one [critic's opinion], particularly if it's a female and you know—God willing, for her sake, I hope it's not the case—but when they get a period, it's really difficult for them to function as human beings.

— **JERRY LEWIS**

Jerry Lewis keeps insisting comediennes are not
funny. . . . When comedians allow ego and bitterness
to overtake them professionally, their comedy
dies. Lewis stopped being funny ages ago.

— **ESTELLE GETTY** (*Golden Girls*)

✳

Who wants to go to the theater to see plays about sex, sodomy,
and substance abuse when you can get all that at home?

— British comedian **PETER COOK**

✳

Yes, Charles Nelson Reilly was in the original cast of
Hello, Dolly! In fact he was the most original one.

— *Dolly!* star **CAROL CHANNING**

✳

Joan Rivers has tried to make it on Broadway. But
in a play, she gives the impression she's annoyed
that the other people onstage get to talk, too.

— **MADELINE KAHN**

✳

Tallulah [Bankhead] was telling me about a theater actor she
knew, . . . an untalented bore and a braggart. He announced,
"I had the audience glued to their seats!" Tallulah responded,
"Dahling, how fiendishly clever of you to think of it!"

— actress **ESTELLE WINWOOD**, who lived to 101

I asked Christopher Isherwood if he intends writing his autobiography, and he said, "I always do."

— Irish interviewer **FIONA CORREGAN**
on the self-referential novelist

✳

He caught me reading a book during a [recording] break, so I asked if he liked Kipling. He looked embarrassed, then said, "I dunno. I've never kippled."

— **MARNI NIXON**, who supplied Audrey Hepburn's
My Fair Lady singing voice, about a Warner Bros. executive

✳

I read where O. J. Simpson said he wasn't going to lower himself to read any of the latest books about him. Lower himself? To do that, he'd have to *climb.*

— director/producer **GEORGE SCHAEFER**

✳

One thing you can say for O. J. Simpson: He never shed a drop of blood except in anger.

— **ROBERT MITCHUM**

✳

I read where recent biographies of Louis Armstrong remove the N-word from his own comments. . . . In *Charlie and the Chocolate Factory*'s new illustrations, the Oompah-Loompahs aren't from Africa anymore. And in the Dr. Dolittle books, they're not only changing words; in some cases they're altering plots. This censorship is like subversion, . . . and doesn't it violate dead authors' rights?

— **DENISE NICKERSON**, Violet in *Willie
Wonka and the Chocolate Factory*

Song of the South [1946] was very popular. I thought it was the best Disney yet. . . . It could have been more racially advanced, but that was long ago. Now they've made it invisible. You can't see it, no how. That's not right.
— African American actress **BUTTERFLY MCQUEEN** (*Gone with the Wind*) to UK writer Ken Ferguson

The Dr. Seuss estate has decided [in 2021] never again to publish or license six of his books that supposedly portray people in ways that are hurtful and wrong. Let the readers judge. Those books were written long ago, and Dr. Seuss earned conservatives' criticism for being ahead of his time. . . . This ban is ludicrous.
— children's book reviewer **CRIS REYNOLDS**

A bully and a bigot, . . . abhorred miscegenation. . . . He loved to kill animals, like giraffes in Africa. Ironically, it's called a Teddy Bear because President Theodore Roosevelt declined to shoot a little bear. It wasn't as fun a challenge as shooting a large or mama bear.
— *New Yorker* staff writer **WILLIAM MURRAY**

Has any celebrity been luckier than Morris? Adopted at a cat shelter 20 minutes before being destroyed, he became spokes-cat for 9 Lives cat food and a media star who ran for president in 1986 as a Democrat. . . . Thank goodness for those who adopt.
— Leading Artists agent **ANN DOLLARD**

A flatworm could write a better script.

— **SYLVESTER STALLONE** denigrating *Stop! Or My Mom Will Shoot!* in which he costarred with Estelle Getty of *Golden Girls*

✳

A heterosexual definitely did that movie, *Deliverance*. When those mountain men rape one of the vacationing canoers, it wasn't Jon Voight or Burt Reynolds or even the plain guy. They chose the fat, ugly one. See it for yourself. No way were the mountain men gay!

— gay book editor **MICHAEL DENNENY**

✳

The old master has turned out another Hitchcock-and-bull story in which the mystery is not so much who done it as who cares.

— *TIME* **MAGAZINE** on *Vertigo* (1958), now widely considered one of the all-time classic films

✳

Sandy Dennis has made an acting style out of postnasal drip.

— critic **PAULINE KAEL**

✳

Ricardo Montalban is to improvised acting what Mount Rushmore is to animation.

— actor/director **JOHN CASSAVETES** on the *Fantasy Island* star

✳

The only moving thing about Charlton Heston's performance was his wig.

— critic **MICK DURSTON**

Charlton Heston is good at portraying arrogance and ambition,
but in the same way that a dwarf is good at being short.
— **REX HARRISON**, Heston's costar
in *The Agony and the Ecstasy*

✳

Method acting's an abomination. The chief lesson
[taught] is complete egotism. . . . Marlon Brando has
been known to place rubber stoppers in his ears so he
cannot hear the words spoken by other players!
— **BORIS KARLOFF**

✳

She's won more Oscars [four] than any other actor . . . for
convincingly portraying heterosexuals and ageing very well.
— biographer **C. DAVID HEYMANN** on Katharine Hepburn

✳

Cal Culver auditioned for a Katharine Hepburn play. She
eventually cast another young actor, Christopher Reeve. Cal
later became a gay porn star as Casey Donovan. . . . After
the audition, Cal asked Hepburn's opinion of his tryout.
She said, "Frankly, I think you lack a certain masculine
quality." Cal thanked her and replied, "Well, that's something
that could never be said about you, Miss Hepburn."
— **MARTIN GREIF**, writer/publisher and friend of Calvin Culver

✳

She has a face that belongs to the sea and the
wind, with large rocking-horse nostrils and teeth
that you just know bite an apple every day.
— photographer **CECIL BEATON** on Katharine Hepburn

I believe Miss Raquel Welch got her good looks from her father. He is a plastic surgeon, isn't he?

— GROUCHO MARX

✴

Raquel Welch says she corrected what she calls her "Latin nose." What the hell is a Latin nose? I am myself a Latin, and my nose is most decorative!

— Argentine actor **FERNANDO LAMAS**

✴

Zsa Zsa Gabor is known for her talk-show appearances, not for any movie appearance. . . . One more facelift, and she'll be sporting a beard.

— PATTY DUKE

✴

Did you see *White Christmas?* Rosemary Clooney was very pretty then. And thin. She still has a lovely voice, also a lovely complexion—only, so much more of it.

— TONY RANDALL (*The Odd Couple*)

✴

If the public didn't know Michael Jackson's family, he'd be passing for white.

— African American singer **SYLVESTER** in *Frontiers* magazine

✴

George Michael tried to make himself over as sort of a WASP-y blond. He was afraid of being known and stereotyped as Greek—you know, "Third World" and unhip.

— music reviewer **VAL HILL** on the singer born Georgios Kyriacos Panayiotou

Yes. He's not quite a dwarf, but Prince does look
like he was dipped in a tub of pubic hair.
— writer **E. LYNN HARRIS** commenting
on another singer's description

✳

Every other celebrity's coming out with a product line—perfume,
pants, cosmetics, workout tapes. . . . Michael Jackson has
his own line of candy: white chocolate with a nut inside.
— comedian **GILBERT GOTTFRIED**

✳

Tallulah was mortified when she played Cleopatra [onstage]
and a critic wrote that being 40-ish, she was too old for the
part. She telephoned a friend renowned for his honesty
and asked, "Dahling, the truth: I don't look 40, do I?"
He answered, "No, Tallulah, you don't. Not anymore."
— actress/companion **PATSY KELLY**

✳

The classic response to a critic was from a French stage actor,
long ago, who wrote a note to a critic who'd slammed him. He
said something like, "I sit in the smallest room in my house.
Your review is before me. Soon it will be behind me."
— filmmaker **RICK MCKAY**

✳

I use negative reviews, of myself and friends and most
coworkers, to line the bottom of my birdy's cage.
— Oscar-winner **CLAIRE TREVOR** (*Key Largo*)

Men are more prone to everything, from gout to color-blindness.
. . . Logically, males should live longer—they don't get
pregnant and bear children, no menstruation, no menopause.
. . . With all that, women still live longer. *That* is strength.

— **MURIEL SIEBERT**, the first woman to sit
on the New York Stock Exchange

*

Clueless young females who chirp, "I'm not a feminist,"
care more about makeup, hair, and texting than
equality and their own human rights. . . . Democracy
is way down on their puny list of priorities.

— actress/activist **OLYMPIA DUKAKIS**, whose cousin
Michael ran for president on the 1988 Democratic ticket

*

Islam decrees that a female cover her head in shame, so
it galls me when they come to Italy and still do that. . . .
I recently confronted a Muslim in whose country it is
illegal not to cover her head in public. She told me since
Italy is a democracy, she is free to cover her head!
I told her that in a democracy, one is also free
to be a Nazi, but one *shouldn't* be!

— journalist **ORIANA FALLACI**

*

I don't believe in the Supreme Court as it is. I don't believe the
setup is right. I don't believe the Supreme Court is large enough.

— **TRUMAN CAPOTE** in 1982

Don Imus is an example of this hateful trend . . . of self-enriching shock-radio hosts' vicious put-downs. How apt that *IMUS* stands for *Integrated Manure Utilization System.*
— non-shock-radio host **LYNN SAMUELS**

✳

George Floyd was a petty criminal. The officer who killed him was an even worse lowlife. But making a *hero* out of Floyd to somehow admire? Only if you need your head examined.
— actress **PAT CARROLL** to reviewer/interviewer Dave Reynolds in 2021

✳

Psychiatrists are where simpleton actors go to feel they're complex.
— Broadway producer **DAVID MERRICK**

✳

Not me, brother. A psychiatrist is a fellow who finds you cracked and leaves you broke.
— **HUMPHREY BOGART**

✳

When a wife commits suicide, people seldom wonder what *he* did wrong or failed to do. . . . But when the husband does, his widow often becomes a focus of suspicion or disapproval.
— Dr. **JOYCE BROTHERS**

✳

I've had female students who got crushes on William Shakespeare because of his love sonnets. I don't necessarily inform them that, for instance, "Shall I compare thee to a summer's day?" was written to a young man.
— high school English teacher **FRANCES BAIRD**

Shakespeare's plays are bad enough, but yours are even worse.

— novelist **LEO TOLSTOY** (*War and Peace*) to fellow
Russian Anton Chekhov after viewing *Uncle Vanya*

✳

This is a terrific script. It just needs a complete rewrite.

— director **PETER BOGDANOVICH** to writer
Alvin Sargent regarding *Paper Moon*

✳

Ernest Hemingway has never been known to use a
word that might send the reader to a dictionary.

— WILLIAM FAULKNER

✳

He created next to nothing—he photographed Campbell soup
cans or took others' photos of Marilyn and Mao and colored
them in with pastels. He had no depth, nothing to say.

— *Vogue* photographer **HORST** on Andy Warhol

✳

When we championed trash culture, we had no
idea it would become the only culture.

— critic **PAULINE KAEL**

✳

I wouldn't pay 25 cents to spit on a Georgia O'Keeffe
painting. And I think she's a horrible person, too.
I know her. . . . So arrogant, so sure of herself. I'm
sure she's carrying a dildo in her purse.

— TRUMAN CAPOTE to interviewer Lawrence Grobel

Pentimento by Lillian Hellman was a best-selling book. The classy movie *Julia* was made from it. Then it came to light that Hellman lied; the whole *Julia* story happened to someone else, not her. . . . Stealing another's life story is not classy.

— novelist **PAUL BOWLES**

✳

The most pernicious gay stereotype in all of television has to be and is Dr. Zachary Smith on *Lost in Space*.

— gay publicist **HOWARD BRAGMAN**

✳

Very fortunate TV actor, Bob Denver. Barely anything to offer, looks-wise and personality-wise. He was Maynard the beatnik, prehippies, on *Dobie Gillis*. Then he lucked out even more— Gilligan! His own island. After that, of course, the luck ran out.

— **BILL LUTZ**, 1960s TV casting director

✳

Rush Limbaugh sneered at the fact that smoking causes cancer. He said people who smoke die, but so do people who eat carrots. . . . He's just announced [at 69 in 2020] that he has late-stage lung cancer. Who's sneering now?

— actor **CHRISTOPHER PENNOCK**

✳

Karen Carpenter became thin enough to be buried in pleats.

— **JOAN RIVERS**

A triumph of the embalmer's art.

— **GORE VIDAL** on Ronald Reagan

I heard a political speech that hit it right on the nose.
History will excoriate the Reagan administration for its moral
weakness in acknowledging or confronting the AIDS crisis.
It's the worst case since Herbert Hoover of a president doing
next to nothing when he should have known better.

— **TOM HSIEH**, member of the San Francisco
Board of Supervisors. Various economists credited
Hoover with enabling the Great Depression.

Well, I'd been Eddie Fisher's wife for many, many months, and to
be perfectly candid, I thought it was finally someone else's turn.

— **ELIZABETH TAYLOR** in 1999, after publication of
Fisher's very unflattering (to his ex-wives) memoirs

I did "'The Hyphen" to criticize what it stands for. . . .
Like my song says, it fans the flames of hatred.

— **JOHN WAYNE**, who recorded a 1973 spoken-word
album that included "The Hyphen," for which he wrote the
lyrics. Among them: "It seems to me when a man calls
himself an 'Afro-American,' a 'Mexican-American,' 'Italian-
American,' . . . what he's saying is I'm a divided American."

I did hear something about that.

— golden-age movie director **GEORGE CUKOR**,
when asked if he'd heard that in the 1950s, John Wayne
was a financial supporter of the Ku Klux Klan

✳

What does a Nazi carry for a good-luck charm? A *rabbi's*
foot! . . . What do Japanese men do when they have
erections? They *vote*! . . . I got a million of 'em.

— alleged comedian **SAM KINISON**

✳

I sicken of the excuse for hating Jews that "the Jews killed Christ."
He was Jewish, and it's like hating the Americans because they
killed Abe Lincoln. Jews at that time were ruled by the Romans—
what we'd now call Italians. Jesus violated unfair Roman law. . . .
But quit, already, with all this hatred, this stupid nonreasoning!

— movie star **DANNY KAYE**, born David Daniel
Kaminsky, to writer Chad Oberhausen

✳

The military at Pearl Harbor was an occupying force. Hawaii
was a territorial possession. . . . The US had stolen the islands
from the Hawaiian people, with help from Mr. Dole, the
pineapple tycoon who had friends in Washington [DC].
America delayed us becoming a state . . . [because] the majority
wasn't Caucasian or Christian. We were the very last, number 50.

— singer **DON HO** in an unpublished interview
("too controversial") for the *Japan Times*

I liked his music, . . . but I must admit I only recall
watching one Elvis Presley movie, *Blue Hawaii*. I was in
it. I played his mother. I believe I was a southerner.
— ANGELA LANSBURY

✳

Somebody once called me a sissy because I'm
polite. . . . There's a *man* in *manners*.
— ELVIS PRESLEY

✳

The most sexist and illogical phrase is *mother of
God*. If God, however you wish to picture God, had
a mother, then that—*she*—would be God.
— HELEN REDDY

✳

They never raised a statue to a critic.
— dance doyenne **MARTHA GRAHAM**

✳

Critics are eunuchs at a gang-bang.
— GEORGE BURNS

13

Hyp, Hyp, Hypocrisy!

Seem what you should like to be, and the
public will be none the wiser.

— **MACHIAVELLI**

David Bowie has one blue eye and one brown eye. Two
colors, which makes sense—he has two faces.

— Monty Python's **GRAHAM CHAPMAN**

I missed slightly. I meant to blow his balls off.

— producer **WALTER WANGER**, who in 1951 shot and injured
agent Jennings Lang in the groin after learning his wife, movie
star Joan Bennett, was having an affair with him. The men's
Hollywood careers weren't harmed by the scandal; Bennett's
was. A serial adulterer, Wanger later produced *Cleopatra*,
starring Elizabeth Taylor, the most expensive movie yet.

I'm against killing. . . . There's too much of that in movies now.

— actor **AUDIE MURPHY**, who killed a record 240
Germans and earned 28 medals in World War II

The raunchy aspect of movies has sort of gotten out of hand.
When it comes to entertainment, I'm kinda conservative.

— **BOB CRANE** (*Hogan's Heroes*), secret
pornographer and film exhibitionist (not exhibitor)

I don't think the point is who really killed Bob Crane. It happened. As a sex addict and serial pornographer, sooner or later a jealous husband would have killed him. He smugly posed as a family man but had sex with countless women and recorded several dozen encounters on film. What do you expect?
— Hollywood historian **KENNETH ANGER**

The current profanity in popular entertainment is needless and tasteless.
— **KATHARINE HEPBURN**, who in her final movie said, "Fuck a duck" (fowl language?)

Everyone thought I'd be gone before my time. . . . Lots of big names you can name, they died young, burned themselves out. . . . I'm still here.
— **JOHN BELUSHI**, denying the drug addiction from which he died at 33

You gotta fight for your country. . . . You gotta go fight and even die if you have to.
— **JOHN WAYNE** during the Vietnam War. Unlike several stars, Wayne didn't fight in World War II. He applied for and received 3-A status. When director John Ford invited him to join the navy, Wayne applied for and got a 2-A classification, a deferment. Later reclassified as 1-A, Wayne sought his studio's help in returning to 2-A status.

Joan of Arc helped expel the English conquerors
who occupied northern France in the Middle Ages.
In reward, she was put on trial, mostly for wearing
men's clothes, . . . then burned at the stake.
— French actress **FRANÇOISE DORLÉAC**

✳

Any nation that employs a so-called morality police
force like Iran does is surely an immoral society.
— **ANONYMOUS IRANIAN ACTRESS** living in Paris in 2022

✳

There have been many accolades uttered about
Elvis . . . through the years, all of which I agree with
wholeheartedly. I shall miss him as a friend.
— **FRANK SINATRA**, upon Presley's death. The older singer was
one of Elvis's biggest detractors, calling the popular newcomer
and his music immoral and a corrupting influence on youth.

✳

Laurence Olivier is ruthless. . . . My father at 64 was experiencing
the onset of Parkinson's. He was good but not at his very best
in *The Master Builder* at the National Theatre. So "Larry"
fired my father, . . . then took over the role himself.
— actor **CORIN REDGRAVE**, son of Sir Michael Redgrave

✳

One of the finest actresses on the screen that I've ever seen.
— **JOAN CRAWFORD** on a British TV talk show,
about Elizabeth Taylor, whom decades earlier
she called a "blemish on public decency"

Kissing [Marilyn Monroe] was like kissing Hitler.

— *Some Like It Hot* costar **TONY CURTIS**, who late in life fabricated an affair with Marilyn for publicity

I did a movie with [John] Wayne and was very surprised to find out he had small feet, wore lifts and a corset. Hollywood is seldom what it seems.

— **ROCK HUDSON**. You should know, Rock.

※

My wife and I can hardly bear to be apart, except when I have to work.

— gay actor **ANTHONY PERKINS**. Though contractually married, Perkins continued seeing men. For instance, in 1976 he took a "bachelor" vacation to Morocco, where he indulged in drugs and underage males. He died of AIDS in 1992. His wife died via the 9/11 terrorist attack in Manhattan.

※

There's a short, allegedly straight "superstar" who lives in partial terror that it might come out that during his earliest days in Hollywood, he was employed by a top male-escort service that serviced men.

— director **GENE SAKS** (*Mame*), ex-husband of Bea Arthur

※

I don't shy away from violence, but all my pictures should have a high moral tone. It's a line I try to follow myself.

— director **HOWARD HAWKS**. Star Norma Shearer told friends how Hawks moved his 16-year-old girlfriend into the house while his wife, Athole, Norma's sister, was ill and confined to bed. The affair continued while Athole's health declined. Howard, who was racist, homophobic, and anti-Semitic, eventually married the girl.

Another political hypocrite down the mortal drain. . . .
Congressman Henry Hyde, in charge of the impeachment
of President Bill Clinton, hid his own extramarital affair.

— journalist and author **ROBERT TIMBERG**

✳

The thought of being president frightens me,
and I do not think I want the job.

— **RONALD REAGAN** in 1973. Years later, Walter Mondale,
running against President Reagan, observed, "You've got
to be careful quoting Ronald Reagan because when
you quote him accurately, it's called mudslinging."

✳

All of my executives are God-fearing family men.

— MGM's **LOUIS B. MAYER**. Shirley Temple's autobiography
divulged that Mayer tried to seduce her 37-year-old mother,
Gertrude, while in an adjoining office, *Wizard of Oz* producer
Arthur Freed exposed his genitals to 11-year-old Shirley.

✳

Man Who Fought against Gay Adoption Molests Child

— 1999 *FAB!* **HEADLINE** about an antigay activist in
Indiana charged with molesting a nine-year-old girl

✳

These fact-challenged activists try and scare parents about
gay teachers supposedly molesting the boys in schools.
They obviously never mention straight [male] teachers
molesting girl students, which is much more common.

— sex therapist **SHIRLEY ZUSSMAN**

You are what you eat.

— nutritionist **GAYELORD HAUSER** (the phrase
made him rich and famous), who advocated yogurt,
buckwheat, and blackstrap molasses and warned against
Italian food. In the 1960s, ex-neighbor Truman Capote
revealed, "Gayelord lived in a castle on a hill in Italy, and
whenever I saw him eating, it was usually pasta."

I love Halloween. Giving candy to all those little kids.
Does my heart good, and I mean that sincerely.

— **BOB HOPE**, who gave away not candy but photos of himself

The public's not going to buy me as an alcoholic.

— movie star **WILLIAM HOLDEN**, declining a 1980s TV
miniseries role. He was in fact alcoholic and died because of it.

Doesn't Ronald Reagan *think* before the words come out of
his mouth? He becomes indignant about Ed Asner finding
fault with his prodictatorship Central America policy and
says, "What does an actor know about politics?" Exactly!
All this ex-actor knows is helping the rich, unhelping the average
American, and heaven help the poor, . . . just carries out the
orders of his corporate and billionaire sponsors and bosses.

— journalist/author **ROBERT TIMBERG**

I remember Ronnie [Reagan] telling all of us not to
join TV because it was the enemy of the movies.
Next thing, he was on *General Electric Theater* with
his contact lenses reading the commercials.
— Warner Bros. star **ANN SHERIDAN**

Jane Wyman's fan magazine PR claimed she was "lonely"
without Ronald Reagan, like millions of wives during World
War II. *The Peter Lawford Story* noted, "The fact that Reagan
slept at home each night was ignored." Fanzines referred
to him being "on leave." Technically he was in the army,
but his "war work" might take him to the Disney studio
in Burbank to narrate an animated film on the war.
— columnist **LEE GRAHAM**. The 1988 book was
cowritten by Lawford's widow. Peter, brother-in-law
to President Kennedy, was pals with actor Robert
Walker, a pre-Reagan boyfriend of Nancy Davis.

If Nancy Reagan were alive, she'd drop mortified dead, being
called the "blow job queen of Hollywood," . . . with all these
revelations about her oral talents while trying to become a name
actress. . . . There's too much evidence to quickly dismiss it.
— news and entertainment publicist **ANDREW FREEDMAN**

✴

Some of my best friends are homosexuals.
— then-actor **RONALD REAGAN**. On being elected
governor of California in 1966, one of his first acts was
to fire two staffers simply because they were gay.

Prince often flirted with a bisexual image, which was daring because he really was bisexual. But when he shifted into movies, his vehicle *Purple Rain* was homophobic. He went right along with that accepted, mean-spirited method of trying to build oneself into a male movie star. Fortunately, he only ever made two flicks.

— actor **LOUIS ZORICH** *(Mad about You)*

"Uncle Walt" wanted the public to like him. Employees didn't count, and of course he took public credit for much of their work. The most praise a noncelebrity Disney employee could expect was his phrase *That'll work.*

— **HAL GAUSMAN**, set decorator on *Mary Poppins*

You never saw Walt Disney without a mustache. He didn't have much identity without it. . . . His male employees weren't allowed to wear mustaches.

— **JOANNA BARNES** *(The Parent Trap)*

I believe in all-American, good, decent moral values.

— celebrated golden-age movie director **FRANK CAPRA**, who also believed in anti-Semitism

I don't hold with bigotry, and anyone at all who can afford it is welcome to stay in my hotels.

— **CONRAD HILTON**, at a time when hotels could legally refuse service to other colors, religions, and nationalities. Hilton bypassed sister-in-law Eva Gabor's wedding because the bridegroom was Jewish.

When Hollywood did the movie of the play *The Diary of Anne Frank* with Susan Strasberg, they dumped her for an unknown non-Jewish actress. The reasoning? Middle America might be turned off, threatened, whatever, if a Jewish actress plays a Jewish character.
— Jewish actor **ROD STEIGER**, quoted in the *Jewish Journal*

I taught my son to cherish and respect his [Jewish] heritage.
— **SADIE BERLE**, who changed her first name to Sandra in the 1950s when her son Milton Berle become a TV comedy star

It made me giggle when my uncle sued [in 1999] over an unauthorized photo of him as Carmen Miranda. He felt his manhood was threatened. But his most famous comedy shtick was getting into a dress and lady's hat and wearing high heels sideways. . . . Then he'd walk crazy, bat his eyelids, and purse his lips. It was hilarious. Now he doesn't think it's funny?
— Milton Berle's actor-nephew **WARREN BERLINGER**

✳

Now it's Italians! He's already slimed Jews and gays, even though he's gay or, at any rate, a pederast. Peter Pansy . . . talk about arrested development—too bad his money keeps him from getting arrested.
— actor **RICHARD LIBERTINI** on Michael Jackson, quoted in *Oggi* magazine

In 1993, Michael Jackson paid $23 million to quickly settle a boy-child molestation lawsuit. A 10th of that, $2.3 million, would have indicated something to hide. But $23 million is sheer panic and terror.
— publicist **HENRI BOLLINGER**

Errol Flynn, after his two rape trials, was more popular than ever. . . . His employers knew O. J. Simpson was a wife beater—it meant nothing to them. . . . Jeffrey Epstein, convicted of soliciting prostitution from girls of even 14 [in 2008], *still* socializes with top politicians and movie stars.
— **MARIA SCHNEIDER** (*Last Tango in Paris*) in 2010. In 2019, Epstein was arrested for sex trafficking of minors; he committed suicide in jail.

My newspapers always enforce a high moral tone. . . . My editorial policy does not condone living in sin.
— exactly what married-man **WILLIAM RANDOLPH HEARST** did, with his mistress, actress Marion Davies. The ultraconservative publisher admired Hitler.

Goodbye, Cardinal Cookie, you're out of the closet at last! That son of a bitch hypocrite. . . . Practically every priest I know is gay. Even the ones that claim they're not. . . . The gay baths in New York, half the clientele are priests.
— **TRUMAN CAPOTE** in *Conversations with Capote* on New York's late, censorious Cardinal Francis Spellman, whose influence was such that the *New York Times* ignored reports of his sexually importuning males

Outing is simply telling the truth. Not about your neighbor or cousin but closeted hypocrites who publicly battle their own kind. . . . Like the so-called ex-gay paid by religious fundamentalists to pretend gay people can "convert" who routinely went to a Washington, DC, gay bar for pickups.
— filmmaker **RICK MCKAY**

I fault the ones who *never* come out. . . . Some now openly lesbian stars have been maligned for their past closeting. But if they hadn't, they wouldn't have been given their big breaks. I can name equally talented actresses and comediennes who have been open and honest from day 1 and have thus never been given their big break. Get famous first, *then* come out. Otherwise, no fame.
— actor-turned-writer **JACK LARSON**

There is more than one new author who, while part of the late Princess Diana's inner circle, publicly described her in glowing terms but now describes her in attention-getting, sales-motivated, unflattering terms, the better to sell a new book. Where is the morality or decency? The only surviving respect is for money.
— UK journalist and broadcaster **ANTHONY HOWARD**

[The characters] readers envy in my books . . . have to come to a bad end, see, because that way the people who read me can get off the subway and go home feeling better about their own crappy lives.
— best-seller **JACQUELINE SUSANN** to her editor after an interview where she praised "my wonderful, sophisticated readers"

It is a hypocrisy for writers to call something a name
that has nothing to do with it when they *know* it has
nothing to do with it and it insults an entire nation.
. . . Calling the international influenza crisis the
Spanish influenza is malicious, a hypocritical lie.

— Spanish movie star **SARA MONTIEL**

✳

The US advertises fairness, . . . yet people of Chinese origin
are attacked on their streets because of COVID. . . . What
about Nigeria's monkeypox? Black Americans are not
attacked for that. No people should be blamed for diseases.

— Chinese Australian writer **KAREN LIU**

✳

My son David was the first AIDS coordinator in Los Angeles.
In his memory, I'm participating in several fundraisers to
help stop AIDS. . . . Those who believe AIDS is God's
punishment believe in a devil, not a god. How do they
explain the Black Death that killed off a third of Europe?

— **RUSSELL JOHNSON**, the Professor on *Gilligan's Island*

✳

Whitney Houston never found her way. . . . Bi or lesbian
but ever in denial. Not "black" enough for some, so she
then engaged in reverse-racist behavior, like at the Grammy
Awards. . . . She used anti-Jewish language. . . . And no,
she wasn't a drug addict. Not till she died from it.

— talent manager **SANDY GALLIN** to columnist George Christy

About Colin Powell, . . . I am not 100 percent against
Republicans, but when you examine the motives
of many black Republicans, you'll sometimes find
excess ambition and hypocrisy. . . . The career, not
the membership, overrides most considerations.
— African American performer/activist **HARRY BELAFONTE**

✳

It's funny how the same people who shrill about too much
government are usually the ones who endorse politicians
who push government into our bedrooms and lecture
us on how to live, love, worship, and reproduce.
— actress **KATHERINE HELMOND**

✳

If marriage is purportedly "for procreation only," then thousands of
heterosexual marriages without children—including those of some
antigay political couples—would have to be legally dissolved.
— actor/playwright **HARVEY FIERSTEIN**

✳

The word *Olympics* has been used for centuries for all manner
of competitions, . . . even races using rats or cockroaches.
Yet we were forced to change the Gay Olympics to the Gay
Games because the International Olympic Committee won
their bigoted and hypocritical lawsuit against us. Since
when does a company or committee own a single word?
Had it been, say, a cockroach Olympics, they
might have refrained from suing.
— Gay Games founder Dr. **TOM WADDELL**

No, it's ours. They should never have it.
— **JOHN WAYNE** on the Panama Canal.
Eventually he supported President Carter's
plan to gradually cede it to Panama.

I love these California hypocrites who are so down on immigration
from south of the border who never stop and ponder, . . .
Who's working in the fast-food restaurants and doing the
cooking and cleaning in the regular restaurants? Who's working
in the fields picking the crops we buy at our supermarkets?
Who's doing most of our gardening? Who takes the jobs other
races avoid and keeps things running on a daily basis?
Stop and *think* . . . at least appreciate who's doing
all this and usually for minimum wage.
— documentarian **ALBERTO DOMINGUEZ**

Yes, I'm Spanish. . . . I was presented at the royal court in Madrid.
— Mexican actress **DOLORES DEL RIO**, cooperating
with 1920s Hollywood publicists, who felt it was classier
to have a European background than a Latin American
one. Del Rio later reclaimed her heritage.

It's inane when half the time that a gay-themed movie comes out,
the director or actor says in interviews it's not *really* gay-themed.
When does anyone say about a straight movie, "It's not *really*
straight"? If they're trying for a bigger audience, then don't make
a gay movie. If you make a gay movie, be honest and be proud,
and don't turn off the gay audience with fictitious hypocrisy.
— journalist **LANCE LOUD**

I'm of Irish origin. . . . I'm from Tasmania, in Australia.

— movie star **MERLE OBERON**. Before celebrity journalism, stars' claims were seldom investigated. Oberon almost certainly never visited Tasmania. Sadly, she had to hide the fact that her mother was Indian (from India). Though Indians are Caucasian, any background originating in Asia was deemed "inferior" to a European one. When she moved to London, Oberon reportedly passed off her darker-skinned mother as her maid.

I took the name from my Russian ancestors.

— **BORIS KARLOFF**, born William Henry Pratt, was also part Indian. His daughter Sara has said she knows of no Russian forebears in her father's family.

The men in Paree, they all go wild for me!

But the men in America, crazee!

— "Parisian" sex symbol **FIFI D'ORSAY**, who'd never set foot in France; she hailed from Montréal, Canada. D'Orsay is now barely remembered for her once-famous catchphrase *Allo, beeg boy.*

A Christmas tradition in our house.

— **DINAH SHORE**, who kept her Jewishness in the closet, instead emphasizing that she was southern, from Tennessee. However, she did choose to be buried in LA's Jewish Hillside Cemetery, with a female rabbi presiding.

Frankly, I think the part's a little too Jewish.

— **DAVID JANSSEN** (born Meyer), declining a part in a 1978 TV movie. The Jewish actor was best known as *The Fugitive.*

Someone becomes a star, they want to appeal to the widest
audience, for the biggest income. . . . What bugged me was
Olivia Newton-John always playing it so white bread. She
was half-Jewish and had a Jewish manager. Her grandfather
Max Born won the Nobel Prize for physics and was a good
friend of Albert Einstein. . . . Who, me, Jewish? Oy!

— Jewish actor **ADAM RICH** (*Eight Is Enough*)

No, I act and direct. . . . Commercials aren't for me.

— **PAUL NEWMAN**, eschewing TV commercials, in
the US. In Japan he did ads for cars and coffee.

Of course I use them. I'm a big believer
in what I choose to promote.

— actress **NANCY WALKER** on her sideline as a paper-towel
salesperson on TV. During a Los Angeles talk show, the *Rhoda* star
let slip, "Sure, . . . my maid uses them every day—I'm pretty certain."

I like it. I listen to disco all the time. . . . It's the new thing.

— **ETHEL MERMAN**, promoting her 1979 disco album.
Privately, she stated, "Why the hell do they call it music for
[*sic*]? This is guano for your ears, for cryin' out loud!"

My looks? . . . I don't think about them.

— **ELVIS PRESLEY**, when asked how it felt being a "handsome
male sex symbol?" He regularly had his lighter-colored hair dyed
a "manlier" black; before his death, he reportedly went gray.

All these celebrities who accepted Jeffrey Epstein's invitations and enjoyed flying around with him in his private jet, . . . now they solemnly intone, yes, wasn't it awful, what a terrible fellow. It was known and on the legal records at the time what kind of a sex criminal fellow he was. . . . Hypocrites!

— **JOHN EMERY**, plastic surgeon and Olympic gold medalist

✴

It's total BS when the kid of a famous actor says he has it as hard or harder than some aspiring actor without a famous parent. There is no comparison. On account of your famous parent, you get to go right in and meet the people who can hire you. The others spend years just trying to meet those people.

— director **EMILE ARDOLINO**

✴

A sound-engineer friend overheard the son of a televangelist say to a visitor in the TV studio what a boring and phony business it was to be in. Yeah, but for years he follows in his preachy dad's very lucrative footsteps.

— attorney **ED FLEISCHMAN**

✴

It's wonderful being Superman. The kids love it, and I love it.

— **GEORGE REEVES** in the mid-1950s. The kids did, anyway. The TV series, aimed at children, effectively banished the former movie actor from the big screen. He also hated his woolen Superman costume.

Playing Superman is a heavy moral weight, so I have to play
nonobjectionable characters in the other movies I do.
— **CHRISTOPHER REEVE**, who later played an
amoral priest blackmailing bishops and having
an affair with a nun in the flop *Monsignor*

Yeah, I think it's a good conception [*sic*]; it's good and moral.
— country singer **TAMMY WYNETTE** on the theme of her
lone crossover hit "Stand by Your Man." However, she married
five times. One of her country hits was "D-I-V-O-R-C-E."

The studios arranged dates for gay stars and used us girls as decoys.
I didn't mind going out with Tab Hunter, though I knew he'd end
up with Tony Perkins, who was assigned his own female date. The
four of us showed up in the limo, camera-ready, paraded into the
cinema while smiling at the flashbulbs, then once inside, after
the lights went out, Tab and Tony got up and went off together.
The girl and I stayed and watched the movie. Nobody
ever photographed anyone *leaving* a premiere.
— **DEBBIE REYNOLDS**

Hypocrisy, thy name is Hollywood.
— **SEVERAL CELEBRITIES**

ABOUT THE AUTHOR

Boze Hadleigh is the author of 30 books, most of them Hollywood-themed. The *Los Angeles Times* labeled him a "pop culture phenomenon." He has a master's in journalism, speaks five languages, has visited more than 60 countries, and won on *Jeopardy!* His non-Hollywood books include *492 Great Things about Being Italian*, *Broadway Babylon*, *Life's a Pooch*, and *Holy Cow!*